# Contemporary Western Ethnography and the Definition of Religion

Continuum Advances in Religious Studies

Series Editors:
Greg Alles, James Cox, Peggy Morgan

*Contemporary Western Ethnography and the Definition of Religion*, M. D. Stringer
*Fourteen Contemporary Theories of Religion*, Michael Stausberg
*A New Paradigm of Spirituality and Religion*, MaryCatherine Burgess
*Religion and the Discourse on Modernity*, Paul-François Tremlett

# Contemporary Western Ethnography and the Definition of Religion

M. D. Stringer

continuum

Continuum International Publishing Group
The Tower Building                          80 Maiden Lane
11 York Road                                Suite 704
London SE1 7NX                              New York NY 10038

www.continuumbooks.com

First published 2008

British Library Cataloguing-in-Publication Data
A catalogue record for this book is available from the British Library.

ISBN-10: HB: 0-8264-9978-3
ISBN-13: HB: 978-0-8264-9978-3

Library of Congress Cataloguing-in-Publication Data
Stringer, Martin D.
    Contemporary western ethnography and the definition of religion / M.D.
Stringer.
        p. cm.
Includes bibliographical references and index.
ISBN-13: 978-0-8264-9978-3 (HB)
ISBN-10: 0-8264-9978-3 (HB)
1. Anthropology of religion–Great Britain. 2. Great Britain–Religion. I. Title.

GN470.S77 2008
306.6′0941–dc22                                              2007027415

Typeset by YHT Ltd, London
Printed and bound in Great Britain by Biddles Ltd, King's Lynn, Norfolk

# Contents

# Foreword

## Chatting to Gran at her Grave

In November 2003 I visited China as part of a small delegation from the University of Birmingham's Department of Theology and Religion. We toured the country, visiting a number of university departments of philosophy or religion. We prepared three papers beforehand, and invited each host to choose one paper to be presented to them in their institution. One of my papers, 'Chatting to Gran at her Grave', addressed the question of popular religiosity in Britain, and explored how British people engage with the dead. This paper proved to be by far the most popular of those we presented to the Chinese. It was the one chosen most often, and talked about most excitedly, by our hosts. This was because I was describing residual religious practice in a modern Western capitalist society and also, I believe, because it spoke so personally to many of the students in our audience. In fact, at one university it was the first time in my life a student left a lecture in tears. When asked what had touched him so much, he told my colleague he had watched his own grandparents undergoing similar rituals, which he had been taught to dismiss as 'ignorance' and 'superstition'. Now, in my lecture, he found a Western scholar who not only legitimated but also celebrated the actions of his grandparents. It was a very emotional experience for him.

Over the past half-century or so there has been a steady stream of books, papers and theses discussing the nature of British religion, or religion in Britain. The vast majority of these have addressed questions resulting from the decline in attendance at mainstream Christian churches. This decline has been known for many years, and its interpretation has led the ongoing debate. Summarizing the debate crudely, we could say that discussion up to the end of the 1980s focused on possible reasons why church attendance was declining so fast. This became known as the 'secularization' debate. From the early 1990s onwards, however, the debate changed subtly with scholars lining up behind either Grace Davie (1994) who, in a now classic text, argued that the prevalence of religion in Britain had not declined, but rather its nature had changed; or Steve Bruce (1995), who used the statistics to show that not only had church attendance declined, but all other measures of religiosity were going in the same direction. More recently the argument has changed again, with a particular focus on the role of women within this decline (Brown 2001). It is not my intention in the present text to get caught up in this wider argument.

This particular work began with an attempt to bypass the wider debate. I am very wary of the argument, based primarily on Davie's work, which suggests that the nature of religion has changed. I am even more wary of the starkness of Bruce's statistical vision. My main interest for some years, coming from a starting point of concern for Christian worship, has been primarily in those who have continued to attend church, and the religion of minority mainstream Christians in our society has been my primary focus. My dogged determination in pursuing this interest, when all around me were becoming more interested in new spiritualities, alternative religions, Charismatic or Pentecostal churches, the 'New Age', raves, or whatever, kept me looking at the rump of the population who continued to identify themselves as Anglicans, Methodists, Catholics or United Reformed Church members. It is these people, primarily, who populate this book. I was surprised to find that, firstly, far from being set apart by their commitment to traditional churches, such people were not very different from their neighbours; and, secondly, that traditional churchgoers did or believed things that many scholars might consider 'alternative' or 'superstitious'.

This discovery, supported by the detailed ethnographic work of my postgraduate students over the years, led to my paper for the Chinese universities, and subsequently to this book. I do not want to argue here for a significant change in religious practice or belief in British society, from traditional church-based religions to new or alternative spiritualities. I do not even want to argue for an increase in pluralism (although this has undoubtedly occurred in British society). My argument here is one of continuity in an *underlying religious sensibility* that was hidden when mainstream Christianity was the dominant religion of our society, but which is now being revealed by the retreat of traditional Christianity, and subsequent changes among ordinary, committed churchgoers. I will argue in my conclusion that in studying religion in Britain we have fundamentally misunderstood the nature of 'religion': to understand what is going on, we need to go back to first principles.

This work would not have been possible without the contributory work of many of my research students – those whose work is quoted, and the many others who are not mentioned by name. As I suggest in Chapter Two, it is no longer possible for one academic to undertake enough primary fieldwork to make any kind of meaningful generalized statements about religion in Britain, or very much else. I have been very lucky in being able to attract a number of high-quality postgraduate research students over the years who have been keen to undertake ethnographic fieldwork of their own in many different communities, and this has produced a set of data that is invaluable to the wider study of religion, as I hope to demonstrate in what follows. I need to pay tribute to my students therefore, and to thank them for their primary research and for their contributions to countless seminars and discussions in which much of the material for this book has been aired.

Beyond the students, I must also acknowledge the contribution of all those people who made up the various communities studied by the students. Each project was collaborative in its own way, drawing on the active participation and cooperation of those being studied, so these people have probably contributed as much to the ideas contained in this text as the students or myself. In my own fieldwork I must also recognize the place of the Ardwick Deanery Young Families Project and the work of Fr Dowden, the other clergy of the Deanery, and the people of East Manchester who established and worked with the Project. As project worker for five years, I found that research was a central part of my brief, and some of the material from that fieldwork has been included in this text. Listening to the young mothers and the older women of the Ancoats, Ardwick and Gorton areas of inner-city

Manchester opened my eyes to the possibilities of a different way of understanding religion and religious practice. This listening has seen its fruition in the theories outlined below.

I must also acknowledge the contribution of those who, in more recent years, have commented on parts of this text in a number of different contexts. I am grateful to the *Journal of the Anthropological Society of Oxford* for permission to republish a version of my paper 'Towards a situational theory of belief' as Chapter Two. My colleagues Edmund Tang, Hugh McLeod, Werner Ustorf, Ian Draper, Gordon Lynch and Matthew Guest have all contributed in different ways to discussions and conversations about this material. I am also grateful to colleagues at the BSA Sociology of Religion Study Group, the Open University, Durham University, the University of Portland and, of course, people of the various universities in China who listened to papers based on elements of this work. I have welcomed and hopefully engaged with their many responses and critiques, although I recognize that any failings that remain within the work are entirely my own. Greg Alles, James Cox and Peggy Morgan, the editors of the series 'Continuum Advances in Religious Studies', and the staff of Contiuum, have also made a significant contribution to the final text, and I am very grateful for their professionalism and encouragement. I also offer my gratitude to David, who has had to live with 'Chatting to Gran at her Grave' in various forms over the years, and without whom I would probably write very little.

Finally, I would like to dedicate this work to my father, who died during its final stages. I am not sure that he ever fully understood why I was interested in the strange activities of ordinary people in graveyards and, as always, he maintained to the end a healthy scepticism about my more theoretical assertions. I hope he would have been amused and intrigued by this final text.

*In memoriam* Peter Stringer, 1927–2007

Chapter One

# On Defining Religion

There are almost as many different definitions of religion as there are people who try to define it (J. Z. Smith 1998: 281). We can define religion, for example, in terms of its function: it is there to answer people's most fundamental needs (Arnal 2000: 24–5). We can define religion in terms of its content: it is belief in supernatural entities (Spiro 1966: 96). We can define religion in terms of the elements it consists of: belief, ritual, faith, etc. (Southwold 1978: 370–1, Smart 1989: 10–21). We can even argue that religion as a concept has no inherent content and is therefore beyond definition (Braun 2000). Each of these approaches, and many more, have been tried and argued over the centuries (Strenski 2006, Arnal 2000). Each has certain factors that make it appealing and most, to some, have elements that make them unsatisfactory.

What unites these definitions of religion, however, is that they tend to be based primarily on intellectual reflection. They originate in the questions asked by scholars. What is religion? What kind of thing is religion? How is it possible to distinguish that which is religion from that which is not religion? And so on. What is more, these questions also, in their turn, make assumptions about the nature of religion before we even begin to move on to the answers. This kind of thinking and questioning is particularly current in Western intellectual traditions where the need to define, confine and manipulate ideas is central. We have to grasp hold of religion in our minds before we can begin to do anything further with it (Spiro 1966).

Two other features of this Western, or perhaps we should say 'Christian', thinking on religion are also worth noting. First, there is an implicit assumption that religion is one thing, that there is a 'thing' out there that can be called religion. In practice, of course, there may not be only 'one' thing called religion, there may be many 'religions' (J. Z.

Smith 2000: 39–43). However, in saying this it is assumed that each of these 'religions' is distinct and coherent in and of itself, and that each distinct 'religion' can be compared with all the other religions in a discipline called 'religious studies' (Braun 2000: 14–15, Capps 1995, Sutherland 1988). The second assumption is that religion is essentially an intellectual activity. It has to do with the higher things of life. Belief is held, at least implicitly, to be superior to ritual. Values and morality are more important than prayer and devotions. Religion is about higher ideals: selflessness, generosity, altruism and so on. This is implicit in many Western discourses on religion, and is difficult to distance from any academic definition of what religion is.

This kind of discourse, however, is rooted in Protestant Christianity (Dubuisson 2003) and has a tendency, less often vocalized today than in the past, to judge all other 'religions' in relation to this Protestant ideal (Masuzawa 2005). Buddhism is good. Hinduism is suspect, except in its intellectual traditions. The work of theologians is good. The so-called 'superstitious' practices of ordinary believers are generally not worthy of our attention. We perhaps pretend that this is no longer the case in contemporary academic discourses, but any attempt to argue the opposite, I suggest, immediately raises these old prejudicial views.

I am not a theologian. I am not even a practitioner of religious studies. My own background is in anthropology and it is as an anthropologist, one who studies living communities going about their everyday activities, that I approach the concept of religion. Anthropology as a discipline has been interested in questions of religion from the early years of the discipline in the nineteenth century (Morris 1987, Strenski 2006). Frazer, Tylor, Spencer, Durkheim and others writing in the late nineteenth century, all addressed questions of religion. These authors, however, rarely went out to study religion in practice, and many of their ideas followed the pattern that I have already outlined. Later writers within the discipline began to approach the questions raised by religion from significantly different perspectives, and it is these assumptions that I inherited from my own study of the subject. However, if we look carefully at the definitions of religion produced even by anthropologists then, I would argue, we come up against the very same principles that are inherent in other definitions. It is the Christian, 'coherent', 'transcendent' and 'transformative' nature of religion that is highlighted over the superstitious, the disordered, the pragmatic and the immanent (Gellner 1999).

Contemporary anthropologists pride themselves on studying real people and developing their theoretical ideas from the detailed long-term study of ordinary people going about their ordinary lives in different parts of the world. Their theory grows out of the field experience and is developed in order to understand and make sense of that field experience. This should also be true of their understanding of religion. In most cases, however, this is simply not the case. My purpose in this book, therefore, is to rectify this error and to base my own thinking about definitions firmly on the fieldwork undertaken by my students and myself. I aim to rethink how 'religion' might be based on the study of real English people going about their everyday religious lives in real places and at real times. Before entering into the fieldwork, however, I need to go back to the wider question of definitions and I need to support the bold, and so far unjustified, statements that I have been making in this introduction.

## Definitions

When I teach an introductory course on 'The Anthropology of Religion' to first-year university students, I always stress the futility of getting caught up in questions of definition. 'Religion' is one of those words that are practically impossible to define in any final sense (Braun 2000). It is a word that is useful to us in specifying a certain kind of thing that we all know when we see it, but any attempt to be precise and nail the definition down to certain key elements is always problematic. So why do I wish to write a book on the 'definition' of religion? One reason is simply to demonstrate the point that I make to my first-year students: that any attempt at definition is futile. More significantly, however, I think that it is actually impossible for any academic to get away from definitions entirely. As anthropologists we do not go into the field without any prior knowledge, observe people doing whatever they might be doing, and then think 'I will call that religion'. We go with preconceptions and implicit understandings that have been more or less formed through detailed study of other authors, and we go expecting to see things that we might want to label 'religion'. In doing this, however, I suggest that we miss what is really going on, we do not see the 'religious' because of what we have inadvertently labelled as 'religion'. It is this label that concerns me in this opening chapter.

When we look at other definitions, we see that there are many different ways into the subject. We can look at the history and use of the concept (Strenski 2006). If we do this we find that 'religion' as we understand it today only really goes back three or four hundred years (J. Z. Smith 2000: 39–42). Talal Asad (1993), for example, reminds us that 'religion' was invented within the turmoil of the 'wars of religion' that raged across Europe following the Reformation. The term was further distinguished from 'theology' during the Enlightenment, and finally came to be applied to 'other religions' and ultimately to 'world religions' within the context of the social sciences in the nineteenth century. It is only in the twentieth century that something that could be called 'religious studies' became a discipline in its own right (Dubuisson 2003). In its history, therefore, religion is seen in opposition to Christianity or to Christian theology: it is a negative term, a term that claims primarily what it is not, rather than what it might be (Braun 2000: 8).

If we cannot use the history of the word itself, therefore, as a useful guide to its definition, can we look at the variety of definitions? Gilbert Lewis in his book *Day of Shining Red* (1980: 6–38) provides an interesting analysis of the word 'ritual' and the different ways of defining the word. This could, therefore, be a good starting point for our discussion. He begins by questioning whether ritual is a thing set apart from other things in the world, or whether it is an aspect of many things, particularly actions or performances. The fruitlessness of this debate leads him to suggest that anthropologists generally recognize ritual when they see it, and that it might make sense to look at what Lewis refers to as the 'central area of common agreement' (7) and its periphery or boundaries, that is at those aspects that all things generally recognized as 'ritual' have in common, before looking at those things which lead anthropologists to question whether a thing is ritual or not. Finally Lewis looks at the relationship between ritual and language, and asks whether ritual is always communicative or sometimes merely expressive. Apart from this final debate, the same kind of questions could be asked of religion as Lewis asks of ritual, probably with much the same inconclusive answers.

Finally we could look at other definitions and see what kind of intellectual framework the definitions of religion actually work within. This is where I began, and it is in relation to the definitions of others that my initial critique is most apparent. I have suggested that the definitions that have developed, even within the anthropological and sociological literature, have been heavily dependent on certain pre-conceptions within a series of Western discourses that are essentially underpinned by Protestant Christianity. We could, if we wished, trace the historical roots of these ideas through Protestant theology, German philosophy and into the social sciences via Marx, Weber and others (Morris 1987: 5–90). Even the alternative roots, through French anti-clericalism and Comtian rationalism, through to Durkheim and his followers (Morris 1987: 106–22), can also be seen to have their fundamental starting point in a Protestant rejection of later medieval Christianity (Milbank 1990). It is not my intention, however, to trace this history in every point of its detail. My proposition is that through these histories all contemporary definitions of religion (whether explicit or implicit) within the social sciences have three features in common: they treat religion as a unified object; they assume that religion is associated with the transcendent; and they see religion as fundamentally transformative for the individual and/or society. These are all, I would propose, elements associated with Protestant theology and all owe their roots, ultimately, to this source. Let me, therefore, look at each one in turn.

## That Religion is One

As we have already seen, the word 'religion' in the context of the gradual acceptance of a range of so-called 'world religions' assumes that each 'religion' is a single coherent whole with a clear and consistent stance that makes it distinctive and different from all the other 'religions' (J. Z. Smith 2000: 39–43). It is therefore assumed, within disciplines such as religious studies, that we can talk about 'religions' and that these can, more or less, be easily defined or at least distinguished one from another. This is not, however, the particular form of definition that I wish to explore within this section. While it is certainly true that the idea of 'religions', each being complete and coherent in itself, was for a while taken for granted within anthropology, this has never been a significant part of the discourse on religion. Even E. E. Evans-Pritchard's famous work *Nuer Religion* (1956), which presented the religious ideas of the Nuer people of southern Sudan as a coherent whole, modelled on Evans-Pritchard's own understanding of Catholicism, is not really arguing for Nuer religion to be placed alongside Islam, Catholicism or Buddhism as another kind of religion (v–ix). Evans-Pritchard's argument is more subtle than that, although many of the protagonists for so called 'African religions' or 'traditional religions' have tended to interpret Evans-Pritchard's work in this way (e.g. Idowu 1973).

In order to get at the idea of unity that I am critiquing, we can begin by looking at Evans-Pritchard's classic work in more detail. It is clear that he listened carefully to what the people around him were saying, and managed to gather a great deal of evidence for a range of spiritual entities that populated the Nuer world. He also observed a series of rituals that engaged with these entities, and entered into a certain amount of abstract discussion with the Nuer. The proposal, however, that all these entities could be seen ultimately as 'one', a single form of *kwoth* 'refracted' through many different forms (*kuth*, the plural form of *kwoth*), is far more than could sensibly be sustained by the evidence he collected (Evans-Pritchard 1956: 91). The fact that the Nuer use the same term for all forms of Spirit should not be taken as implying that the Nuer see all these spirits as refractions of the same entity (any more than the English use of the word 'spirit' does for us). The language Evans-Pritchard uses, while obviously trying to avoid specifically Catholic terminology, is so reminiscent of attempts to explain the classic three-in-one dilemma of the Christian Trinity that we can clearly see his own hand in his unifying doctrine. What, ultimately, is wrong with a people engaging with a whole series of different spiritual entities depending on the pragmatic realities of the different situations in which they approach them? There is no necessity, and no real evidence, for the spirits of the air and the spirits of the river to be treated by the Nuer as being of the same kind, let alone as aspects of the same entity. It is the anthropologist who has the need to explain.

In different ways other anthropologists have gone down the same track as Evans-Pritchard and attempted to present the disparate and pragmatic beliefs and rituals of the people they have studied as part of a coherent whole. The symbolists and structuralists, who primarily studied the religious activities of peoples from Papua New Guinea, are clearly guilty of this in many different ways. Following Victor Turner's work on the Ndembu (1967) and his desire to find a meaning for every symbol, and, by combining symbols, to construct a series of meanings for every ritual, other 'symbolist' anthropologists have tried to interpret and decode the highly elaborate rituals of New Guinea. Even an author such as Frederick Barth (1975), who has a far more subtle understanding of meaning than Turner, and a clear view of what real ethnographic study is about, ended up looking for a coherence and unity within the male initiatory system of the Baktaman which was clearly not there, and which the people themselves actually denied. He went through the initiations himself in order to discover or provide the missing coherence, and ultimately accepted the possibility that real knowledge was known only to the ancestors (102). What was essential for Barth, however, was that some kind of ultimate knowledge, a series of ideas which drew all the symbols and their meanings together, was knowable, even if no living Baktaman could actually know it.

Structuralism also has this implicit sense of unity within its own attempts to critique the meanings of symbols and rituals. For Claude Lévi-Strauss (1978) that unity may actually go beyond the specifics of a particular religious discourse, or the myths that it may contain, to a unity of the human mind that is common to all humanity. The sense that somehow the structuralist method enables the anthropologist to engage with a series of very disparate sets of data and construct some kind of unity or unified narrative out of that diversity, actually sits at the heart of the structuralist project (Leach 1976). The unity that is discovered may be a deep, consciously constructed unity, but the anthropologist still cannot accept the idea that the myths, rituals and symbols experienced in the field could be a random, unintelligible mess.

Finally, therefore, in this section I want to come to some of the classic 'definitions' of religion within anthropology, such as those of Durkheim and Geertz, to see just how important the sense of the unity of religion is to these core texts. Emile Durkheim's definition begins with 'Religion is a unified system of beliefs and practices ... ' (1995: 44) and even Clifford Geertz has 'Religion is (1) a system of symbols which acts ... ' (1966: 4). Both begin their definitions with the idea that religion is a 'system'. This may not imply that they think it is 'systematic' in a theological sense, but the idea that it is a coherent and unitary entity is part of the sense that both these definitions are intended to convey.

## Awe and the Supernatural

The most famous presentation of religion as transcendence is, without doubt, Rudolph Otto's work *The Idea of the Holy* (1928). Otto focuses on the idea of the numinous and then goes on to identify elements of the numinous as '*mysterium tremendum*' (12–24) and 'fascination' (31–41). Otto was, of course, writing within a self-professed Protestant Christian tradition so it is not surprising that he developed this approach. He was not, however, the only writer to explore the question of transcendence as the defining feature of religion.

Evans-Pritchard in his book *Theories of Primitive Religion* (1965), an investigation into the early history of the study of religion in anthropology and other social sciences, uses the label 'emotionalists' of a whole school of theorists who, in their different ways, took the idea of 'awe' or 'wonder' as the starting point for religion (31–46). These writers, as with many nineteenth-century scholars, were attempting to explain the origins of religion, and the key feature for all these authors was the sense of awe that human beings have at something that is greater than themselves, be it a mountain or other feature of the landscape, the sun, stars and moon, or just their sense of isolation in the vastness of the world. This led writers such as Robert Lowie (1936) to argue that all religion has its origin in the response of awe, and even to argue later in his book that any sense of 'amazement or awe' in response to that which is 'Supernatural, Extraordinary, Weird, Sacred, Holy, [or] Divine' is fundamentally religious (322). Taken to these extremes the idea of awe as the root definition of religion cannot be sustained, and for much of the rest of anthropological history the emotionalist approach to religion was largely abandoned.

It was not just the emotionalists, however, who held the view that the core definition of religion had to do with that which is transcendental, or something bigger than the individual. Even the other main tradition that Evans-Pritchard identifies, the intellectualists (1965: 23–9), could not get away from this idea entirely. We might, for example, take Edward Tylor's classic definition that religion is about 'belief in Spiritual Beings' (1871: I, 383). Tylor had great difficulty with terminology (Stringer 1999b). He simply did not have the language that he needed to express the ideas that he was trying to develop, and where he did have the words he would have liked to use, others had already taken them. His choice of the word 'animism' for the most fundamental form of religion is a good example. He was forced to place the emphasis on the 'soul', the animus, rather than the 'spirit', as he would have preferred, because the 'Spiritualists' had already taken the word that he wanted to use (Tylor 1871: I, 385). The word 'spiritual' is also an unfortunate but largely necessary choice. Durkheim, for example, immediately assumes that Tylor's spiritual beings 'must be understood to mean conscious subjects that have capacities superior to those of ordinary men' (1995: 27), and a number of subsequent scholars have turned Tylor's 'spiritual beings' into 'supernatural' or 'superhuman' entities (Spiro 1966: 91). As I will argue in my conclusion, however, the 'super' element was never really part of Tylor's own conception. Despite this, by using words such as 'spiritual' or 'supernatural' many of the classic definitions have continued to maintain the sense that religion is about that which is above and beyond the merely human.

Even Durkheim, perhaps the least 'emotionalist' of theorists in Evans-Pritchard's terms, still resorts to the idea of the transcendent in his own theory of religion. Put very simply, Durkheim argues that people must worship something greater than themselves (1995: 220–25) and, as he did not accept the idea of a 'god' or any other 'supernatural' entity, Durkheim effectively argues that the only thing greater than the individual is society itself, and so, in worship, people worship society. At the core of this analysis is the view that in worship, or ritual, people are aware of and interact with something that is 'greater than themselves', something transcendent. Because of this it has been argued that Durkheim is in fact an emotionalist (see Ramp 1998), but that is not the purpose of my critique: it is the importance of the something greater, the transcendent, in his analysis that I wish to highlight.

Finally, we could look at the work of Peter Berger and Thomas Luckmann. Whether these authors can be treated as anthropologists or sociologists is a moot point, but not really relevant to this discussion as the theories that they propounded have been extremely influential in the development of both disciplines. In *The Social Construction of Reality* (1966) they argue for a process of externalization, institutionalization, legitimation and internalization for religious ideas such that all religion is seen as socially constructed. However, in the process of transmission from one generation to the next, religion takes on an aura of factuality and legitimacy that is taken for granted by the second generation who, in turn, internalize it through their socialization. Religion, or religious ideas, in these terms may not begin life as 'transcendent' in and of themselves. However, within a generation or two, through a process of institutionalization and legitimation, that is clearly how they are perceived. So, once again, we see that the transcendent is central to the understanding of religion.

What we have seen, therefore, is that in many different definitions of religion, emerging from different traditions, we always come back to the concept of the transcendent, that which is greater than, over and above, the individual. Many anthropologists have over the years critiqued this idea in relation to specific studies, but this is usually done in relation to particular local traditions and what might at one time have been described as 'superstition' as opposed to 'religion'. They have often left the idea of religion itself intact. It is to local traditions, therefore, that I want to turn in my third definitional theme.

### Transformation

*Unity* and *transcendence* are two aspects that we would expect to find in most definitions of religion. The idea of transformation appears to be more marginal and less applicable in most definitions. While the idea of transformation is rarely explicit in definitions it is, I would argue, implicit in many. By 'transformation' I am describing the idea that religion is supposed to change either the individual or society. It may not be entirely clear what kind of change is expected, or the process by which this change takes place, but some kind of change is almost always assumed for a religion to be fully recognized as such.

We could relate this, at a purely practical level, to the theories that followed on from Arnold Van Gennep's work *The Rites of Passage* (1960). Van Gennep defined rites of passage as those rituals that either marked or initiated a change in the individual or society. So rites of passage accompany changes within the life-cycle, they mark changes in the seasons, they perform initiatory functions in relation to secret societies or age groups, and so on. It is the change in the individual and, in Van Gennep's understanding, in the society to which that individual belongs, that is central to these rites. Theories on rites of passage have developed over the years with the work of Victor Turner on initiation and healing (1967, 1968, 1969), various more general works on initiation (La Fontaine, 1985), questions about ritual and time (Leach, 1966b), and so on. Change is one of the 'functions' that a certain strand of ritual theory takes for granted as being central to a certain type of ritual. Audrey Richards' work on the Chisungu ritual from Zimbabwe perhaps makes this most explicit in stating that, in the view of the women involved in it, the ritual 'made' women out of the girls who took part (1956). It is the ritual that performs the task and makes the change.

This kind of literature, however, understands change in a very specific and pragmatic way. Following the ritual, things are simply not the same as they were before. What is lacking in much of this literature is any moral association with the idea of change. The initiated adult in the society is not, per se, better than the child, just different. The performance of a new-year party does not change the moral relationships between the participants; it simply marks a change of date (although here I would question whether a moral element does in fact begin to emerge). What I am trying to suggest, however, in noting 'transformation' as a central element of definitions of religion is that many definitions assume that religion brings about some kind of moral change, that religion is good for the individual or society.

We could, for example, look at the idea of 'salvation'. This is not an idea that anthropologists have tended to focus on (but see Spiro 1966: 92), but is central to the arguments of those who study comparative religion or inter-religious relations. It is assumed that 'salvation', some kind of ultimate goal, is central to all the major world religions. There is a sense of purpose inherent in the religion that drives the individual to improve their performance of that religion, or to improve their moral character. Mark Heim (1995) questions whether the meaning of 'salvation' is the same in all religions and argues that we may have to look for different kinds of goal in each of the major world traditions. However, even he recognizes that 'salvation', the presence of some kind of goal with clear moral overtones, is central to the understanding and performance of all 'real' religions.

It is this question of 'real' religions that takes us back into the anthropological literature. When we look at the anthropological study of communities who in theory practise one of the major world religions – Christianity, Islam, Buddhism – then we see an argument that is rooted in the idea of religion as transformation.

Within each of these contexts there is a discussion about the relationship between popular or local traditions, and those of the elite, a distinction that originates in Robert Redfield's designation of 'great' and 'little' traditions in rural Mexico (Redfield 1960: 40). In the case of Buddhism, Martin Southwold discusses the relationship between 'village Buddhism' and 'true Buddhism', the Buddhism of the scriptures and that of the monks (1983: 1–8). In the case of Islam, the distinction is between 'popular' and 'orthodox', or whatever terms are chosen (Morris 2006: 77–111, Varisco 2005: 4–6). This kind of distinction recognizes, albeit implicitly, that the 'real' form of each of these religions is goal-orientated, to do with 'salvation', however that is defined, but that for ordinary people other criteria may be more relevant.

In the case of Southwold's work, for example, we can see the question of transformation developed in a very interesting way. Southwold, after studying village Buddhists in Sri Lanka, notes the odd observation, for him anyway, that the local villagers are not at all interested in 'nirvana'. When asked to define Buddhism they emphasize not killing animals rather than any ultimate salvific goal (Southwold, 1978: 66). This initially puzzles Southwold as the transformative, salvation-orientated element of religion does not appear to be present for the villagers, although their non-violence towards animals does assume a particular form of ethical behaviour to be aimed at. It is only when he refrains from killing an insect that crosses his field notes, and experiences a sense of oneness with creation, that he claims to understand what the local people mean (68–9). It is only in following a personal conversion experience, as he himself recognizes, that the religion of the people being studied makes sense. This is despite the fact that his particular experience is probably alien to the people, and not part of their religious discourse at all. Having noted a lack of transformative, salvation-orientated elements in the religious discourse of the people, Southwold has to reintroduce one into his own personal narrative in order to claim any understanding of their 'religion'.

This kind of text is central to many different discourses on religion, and therefore an implicit emphasis on transformation becomes central to the definitions of religion they contain. Another example that brings us back to the question of superstition and 'true religion' in Christianity (a discourse framed on the same basis as that between 'village' and 'true' Buddhism) is that of Robert Wuthnow's study of small groups in America (Wuthnow 1994). Here the researcher implies that the supportive comforting form of the religion of these small groups cannot be seen as real religion because it hardly ever leads to a dramatic change in the lives of the people concerned. Transformation, it appears, sits at the heart of Wuthnow's implicit definition of religion. I will come back to this study in Chapter Five.

## Constructing Definitions

Most definitions of religion within the social sciences revolve around ideas of unity, transcendence and transformation; but this is only half of the argument I want to present in this chapter. The other element is to recognize that this kind of definition implies a Christian starting point (J. Z. Smith 2000: 39–43). There is a long tradition in religious scholarship that has argued that Western thinkers, reflecting on the religious discourses of India, constructed Hinduism as a 'religion' after the model of Christianity (Sugirtharajah 2003, Masuzawa 2005). It is also fairly non-controversial to argue that nineteenth-century writers held in their minds a model of religion based on their understanding of Christianity when they approached other religious discourses, or considered religion in the abstract (Asad 1993). To argue, however, that this model continued through the twentieth century and is still the primary model for most scholarship on religion today, may be seen as pushing the argument too far. This, however, is what I wish to suggest.

Each of the three features that I have presented – unity, transcendence and transformation – are central to the Christian discourse (Stringer 2005: 17–23). The same features can, of course, be seen in Jewish and Islamic discourses, although probably to a lesser extent (the systematic nature of Jewish thinking could be questioned, and the need for transformation that we find in Christianity is less clearly present in Jewish and Islamic thinking). Beyond these traditions, however, the three features begin to be compromised or even to disappear altogether. It is perhaps the need for a systematic account of religion that is most clearly associated with Christianity, and has been most influential in the wider study and definition of religion. Christianity, focused as it is on the credal statements constructed within the Trinitarian debates of the fourth and fifth centuries, has a systematic doctrine as a key feature of its discourse. It is the need to be systematic and coherent that has led, over and over again within Christian discourses, to the definition and condemnation of heresy. It would be almost impossible to think of Christianity without the systematic nature of its theology, although in recent years a number of attempts have been made to question this principle.

This kind of unity or systematization has also been central, as we have seen, to Western descriptions of other religions, as in the 'invention' of Hinduism, and in the sociological and anthropological study of other religious discourses. It is, I would suggest, the Christian model that underpins and drives this need to think of religion as systematic. I could also say the same for ideas of transcendence and transformation, although both of these are arguably found more regularly in non-Christian religious discourses from many different places. It is however, in my view, the central role of these ideas in the definitions of religion developed by scholars from the West which has led to Christian models being imposed on other religions.

If the definitions of religion still widely used by scholars, including anthropologists, continue to use Christianity as their implicit model for the 'ideal religion', then clearly the way in which religious scholarship has constructed definitions is itself flawed. This implies that scholars have entered their studies with a pre-formed understanding of what religion is, and then moulded the empirical evidence that they have found in the field to fit this understanding. To some extent this is, of course, inevitable. We all begin our studies with pre-formed ideas and assumptions about a wide range of issues, and some of these remain unquestioned. However, if religion is what we are claiming to study or define, then surely we must realize that we hold preconceived ideas and that we are able to test these ideas over and against the empirical evidence that we find in the field. That testing has not happened in any significant way in the study of religion, and it is what I am aiming to do in this book.

## The Redefinition of Religion

In this text, therefore, I do not wish to begin with a well-honed and all-inclusive definition of what religion is. Rather, I want to draw on empirical studies of ordinary people engaged in everyday life, and in that context to determine what can be defined as 'religion'. There are two principal problems with this proposal, however. The first is methodological and cannot really be answered in advance, and the second is related to the context for the study.

Beginning with the methodological question, there is clearly a problem in identifying that which is 'religious' in the everyday lives of ordinary people if we do not have some preconceived idea of what 'the religious' is. One answer to this problem would be to investigate what the people concerned actually consider to be religious – to look at the 'demotic discourses' of religion among the groups being studied (Baumann 1996: 10). This is what is done in many of the studies I will be drawing upon. That demotic discourse, however, like the academic discourse, has been heavily influenced by Christianity, so what people claim to be 'religious' may not include that which, under a different definition, we may want to include in the category of the religious. As I have already said, I do not think that there is any easy way out of this problem and my solution is actually to shelve it until we come to reinvestigate the questions of definition in the final chapter, after I have presented the studies.

I am going to begin by stating that, in all that follows, I am not investigating the role of 'religion' in the everyday lives of ordinary people. Rather I am going to explore the role of the 'non-empirical', that which cannot be proved through any accepted methodology, in the thought and actions of a wide range of very different people. This stance is based on Dan Sperber's analysis of symbolism (1974). I will look at this in more detail in Chapter Three, but for the sake of clarity at this stage I need to state the outline of what I mean. Sperber argues that we regularly use statements, 'symbolic statements' in his terms, which cannot be proved using encyclopedic knowledge, knowledge which informs our normal understanding of the world. Sperber uses the example of a community in Africa who claim that 'all leopards are Christians' (*ibid.* 129–34). In Sperber's own terms such a statement is nonsense, and patently wrong. In my terms it is 'unprovable': we have no known method of discovering whether leopards are Christians or Muslims, or whether they have a religion of their own. This is what I mean by 'non-empirical' (Connolly uses the word 'trans-empirical' [1999: 6–7] and Williams uses 'super-empirical' [1999: 54], but these terms have too many associations with the transcendent for my purposes). There are many words and actions that ordinary people use or perform which in Sperber's terms are 'symbolic', and in my terms are beyond ordinary empirical proof. These are the issues I wish to highlight and investigate in this study. I will return to this discussion in my conclusion, when I problematize the non-empirical in itself, but for now I will develop my argument using this term.

The other issue is less complex but equally problematic. If we accept that most academic definitions of religion are based on Christian models, and that most ordinary definitions of religion in Western everyday discourses are also based on Christian models, why undertake a study of the role of the non-empirical in the West in order to discover an alternative definition of religion? Surely all we will discover are the definitions that we started with. There is a clear and respected anthropological tradition of going out to the 'other' in order to raise interesting questions about the 'self', and the definition of religion appears to be a good candidate for this kind of analysis. What we ought to do, according to this logic, is to find somewhere in the world where the traditional Christian models of religion do not hold sway, and see what is going on there, not in the heart of Christian or post-Christian Britain.

There would certainly be some logic in this, although to find a part of the world where religious discourses have not been influenced in some way by Christianity, or by academic discourses based on Christianity, may be very difficult. My principal argument against this logic, however, is that if we can find other kinds of discourse on the religious or the non-empirical in English everyday life, discourses that are not dependent on the Christian model, then surely this challenges the Christian model far more persuasively than if we first explore a religious discourse that has never been influenced by Christianity at all. That provides a good argument for studying the role of the non-empirical within our own society to discover what is really going on.

That final sentence, however, leads me to ask how we could ever discover what is 'really going on', and that is where we must turn to ethnography, the other element of my title, and the second chapter of this book.

Chapter Two

# On Ethnography

The title of this work is 'contemporary western ethnography and the definition of religion'. In the first chapter I discussed the idea of a definition of religion; in this chapter I shall discuss ethnography. Ethnography is not only an important and significant way of studying society, but probably the only way in which we could ever understand the reality of religion as practised by ordinary individuals, so providing a significant redefinition of religion.

Ethnography as a methodology has been developed and used most widely in anthropology (Agar 1980) but more recently it has been used throughout the social sciences (Hammersley 1992, Alasuutari 1995). It requires long-term, total immersion in the social group being studied. It has the merit of encouraging depth of study, a holistic approach and the ability to discover what lies beneath the surface. It has the disadvantage of being very specific, highly subjective and impossible to verify, and focusing on one particular community. Some would say that the disadvantages outweigh the advantages, but I think the converse is true if ethnography is handled carefully (Hammersley 1992).

I came to ethnography as a student of anthropology in Manchester, and chose to use the method for my own study of the perception of worship in four Christian congregations in that city, which formed the basis of my PhD (Stringer 1999a). At that time very little formal work had been done on the way the methodology of ethnography was to be approached, and the traditional process of methodological training within anthropology, by which the student was simply dropped into an alien environment and told to 'get on with it', was still prevalent. I undertook my study of the four congregations in Manchester with little methodological training and I learnt a great deal through my involvement in the process. I spent six months in each of the churches, attending all their worship and whatever other activities I could manage. I got to know the congregations and the people associated with the churches, and I came to understand what was happening in their worship in a new and exciting way (42–60).

Since leaving Manchester and moving into academic work at the University of Birmingham I have been committed to using and trying to understand the methodology of ethnography, and to encouraging my own students likewise. This meant that I had to develop training methods and a deeper understanding of the methodology in order to pass on to others what I had learnt. At the same time many new books with a particular focus on ethnography or participant observation were coming onto the market, and the method was being used by an ever-wider group of disciplines. The method still retained, however, its fundamental advantages and disadvantages. It was in this context that I developed the idea for a collective approach to ethnography that lies behind the current work. Before describing that in detail, however, I want to consider the methodology of ethnography itself. I shall begin by tracing the history of the method, primarily within anthropology, and some of the assumptions that have emerged from that history. I then want to focus on the subjective nature of the method, outlining both the advantages and disadvantages of this subjectivity. I shall also raise some of the ethical questions inherent in a method that clearly interferes in the lives of the people being studied. Finally, I want to come back to the project that I undertook with my own students, which led to the fieldwork that forms the basis for this book.

## The Origins of Ethnography

Let me begin, therefore, with the history. In the nineteenth century scholars from a number of different disciplines were beginning to analyse the nature of society. Some, from a natural science background, were interested in the laws that made society function, laws that it was hoped were comparable to Newton's laws of nature, being applicable everywhere and at all times. Other scholars, from a theological or classical tradition, were interested in the origins of society (Stocking 1995: 17–34). Others again, interested in the travel and exploration that had been undertaken during the previous three hundred years, were interested in the 'other', the alien, the different, the exotic. All three of these strands came together among the earliest anthropologists and sociologists, and can be seen in their work (Stocking 1983). All of these scholars, however, had to depend on the work of others, primarily explorers and in some cases missionaries, to provide the raw data on which they worked. They were 'armchair' scholars, hypothesizing on what was primarily textual data (Stocking 1995: 15–17).

The explorers themselves, however, had gradually devised a method of collecting data about the peoples and societies they 'discovered' that they hoped would provide suitable data for the 'scientific' study of the armchair scholars (Stocking 1995: 84–7). In the same way that biologists and geologists had 'schemes' that enabled them to classify and categorize anything new that they discovered, lists of questions were constructed for explorers allowing them to ask a whole series of pertinent questions of any society that they encountered (Royal Anthropological Institute 1971). The ideological underpinning of these schemes was, of course, that of Victorian Europe and America, and they often failed to accommodate the various alternative ways of living that were 'found' by the explorers; nonetheless, this forms the starting point of the process of ethnography, with questionnaires constructed by scholars and administered by untrained individuals in various parts of the colonial world.

The next stage in this process was the idea of mounting expeditions in which an anthropologist or sociologist would accompany the explorers, much as botanists, geologists and other scientists had in the past (Stocking 1995: 87–114). Such expeditions were put together in the late nineteenth century, and some of the earliest anthropological work was undertaken in the context of such enterprises. By their very nature such expeditions often spent many weeks or months with the people they were studying, simply because it was difficult to move on, but the actual process of data collection was not very different from the schemes presented to the explorers of the past. The process was still one of asking questions according to a pre-ordered list, hoping that every relevant topic would be covered. The only difference was that this was now being undertaken by professional scholars who would be able to go 'off script' and still know what they were talking about, so the diversity and uniqueness of the local societies became more visible than was possible with previous methods.

It was Bronislaw Malinowski who, during the First World War, took this process to its next and final stage, developing what is now known as ethnography (Young 1979, Stocking 1995: 244–66). Malinowski, a Polish national, was in Australia when the war broke out and, being an 'enemy national', was threatened with internment (Young 1979: 4). However, he was offered the possibility of leading a series of expeditions to Papua New Guinea and jumped at the chance. These journeys lasted much longer than anticipated, and Malinowski spent much of 1915 and 1917 on the Trobriand Islands living with the inhabitants (5–6). It was from this semi-enforced, long-term study of the local people that ethnography was born. After Malinowski wrote up his experiences and described what he had discovered, in a series of extremely popular books, the advantages of ethnographic study became abundantly clear. Malinowski had discovered aspects of these people, the interconnections of their lives, their motives and their actions, which simply could not be discovered in any other way (Malinowski 1922).

Following on from Malinowski's work, the tradition of ethnographic fieldwork grew within anthropology to such an extent that, in Britain and America, anthropology became synonymous with ethnography, although technically they were still different disciplines until well into the 1980s. During the period from the end of the First World War to the 1960s anthropologists set out to cover the globe, undertaking intensive fieldwork in many different locations and writing ethnographic accounts of many different peoples (Stocking 1995: 367–426, Kuklick 1991). Four factors, however, that derived from Malinowski's work were central to practically all subsequent fieldwork. First, it was in exotic locations: American anthropologists had a tradition of studying what remained of Native American tribal groups (Cole 1983), but for the most part anthropologists set out for distant lands: Africa, Asia, Latin America and the Pacific. The second factor, linked to distance and the exotic, was the emphasis on small-scale societies. In order to provide a comprehensive account of everything that happens within a community, that community must be relatively small and relatively isolated. Anthropologists therefore headed for rural locations and smallish villages. Third, it was felt that the 'real' traditions of a people, their 'pristine culture', might be found in these more isolated locations rather than in the corrupting environment of the cities. And finally, the search for a 'pure' culture led to emphasis on the elderly within the community, those who could 'remember'. The usually male anthropologists also tended to provide an essentially male-orientated view of the societies that they studied (Okley 1996: 211–14).

John Beattie, writing in 1964, described the underlying purpose of this phase of ethnographic study as being to 'record the mosaic of cultures throughout the world before they were lost to rapid social change and it was too late to study them at all' (22). It was what Edmund Leach likened, in a different context, to butterfly collecting (1966a: 2). These were European scholars recording and 'preserving' the 'other'. What is more, in the case of British anthropology in particular, and also in other national traditions, the ethnographic process was intimately connected to the context of colonialism (Asad 1973, Kuklick 1991: 182–241). E. E. Evans-Pritchard, for example, was sent to southern Sudan by the British colonial government in order to discover how the political process of the natives worked, in order that the government could better control them (Evans-Pritchard 1940: 7–15). This must have compromised Evans-Pritchard's own fieldwork, and there is more than a hint of this in some of his texts, but the result was undoubtedly a series of the most famous ethnographic works ever produced (1940, 1951, 1956). This element of compromise, and the growing concern within the discipline about the way in which Western scholars were describing and defining the cultures and lives of others, eventually led to a thorough rethinking of the whole process of ethnography. In the 1970s and 80s anthropology went through a major identity crisis and the very basis of the discipline, built as it was on Malinowskian-style ethnography, was called into question (Davies 1999). It was the question of subjectivity that lay at the heart of the questioning, and this is the topic that I need to turn to next.

## On Subjectivity

In 1967, 25 years after Malinowski's death, his wife published the diaries that he had kept during his fieldwork on the Trobriand Islands

(Malinowski 1967). This proved to be something of a turning point in ethnography. Here, for the first time, we could see Malinowski's true feelings and opinions of the people who had made his name. The diaries reveal a man obsessed by his health, antagonistic to the local people, and utterly frustrated in his work. This is not the image of the ethnographer presented in Malinowski's own published writings (1922: 6–15). The diaries immediately raised questions about the role of the ethnographer, and that of the fieldworker in the production of ethnography (Pratt 1986). The Malinowski diaries raised the question of 'subjectivity'.

At the beginning of his book *On the Invention of Culture*, Roy Wagner presents a picture of the anthropologist about to embark on his or her first stint of fieldwork (1981: 4–10). The anthropologist has no training as such, except perhaps in the language, and they are dumped, almost literally, in a small village in some remote part of the world. They are lost, alone and helpless: needing to find out quickly how to survive in this alien environment, how to find food and shelter, how to get along with the people they have come to study, how to be an ethnographer. It is in these first few hours and days of embarrassment and uncertainty that Wagner sees the 'invention of culture' by the anthropologist, for the people being studied. The people's 'culture' is constructed out of the anthropologist's own embarrassment at the differences between what she knows and is familiar with, and what she finds so alien and unfamiliar among the people she is studying. Anthropology has always, in some form or another, made a virtue out of 'difference'. The general reason given for studying societies so far away from the ethnographer's own experience is that the ethnographer will see things that the people themselves take entirely for granted, but which are unusual or 'different' for the anthropologist. If the people behaved just like the ethnographer then she would never notice any of the most important elements of their culture: their culture would be too familiar.

However, this emphasis on 'difference' once again places the ethnographer at the heart of the methodology. It is what that specific ethnographer notices as different between their home society and the society being studied that forms the basis for the 'construction' of the new culture, and if the ethnographer were to come from a different society then presumably the culture that is constructed would be different. Whether the ethnographer is male or female, what social class they come from, whether they are English, American, French, or from Papua New Guinea, their own childhood experiences and the different communities they have lived in and travelled through, will all affect the nature of the 'difference' they experience with the society that they study, and so affect the 'culture' that they construct for that society. Can this plausibly be a means for discovering 'truth' (Hammersley 1992: 69–72)?

Another way in which subjectivity dominates the ethnographic process is made apparent in the writing-up of the study, at the other end of the process from that of the fledgling ethnographer in Wagner's example. If the anthropologist has studied some small, remote or isolated community as part of their fieldwork, then it is clear that they will be the only person outside that society who can verify that the information being presented is 'correct'. How can the reader of the finished thesis or monograph have any confidence that what is being presented in the text bears any resemblance to reality? It becomes very clear on reading Malinowski's diaries, for example, that many elements in his books have limited relation to the truth of the lives of the Trobrianders, and are elaborated in order to present a coherent narrative, a clear structure, or a convincing theory (Pratt 1986). Without the diaries we would never know whether Malinowski was telling us the truth. However, many readers of Malinowski's original books took what he said as authoritative and reliable.

In the 1980s anthropologists such as James Clifford and George Marcus began to raise these questions, and to explore the process of writing ethnography (Clifford and Marcus 1986). Renato Rosaldo, in a paper in Clifford and Marcus's book, introduced the concept of 'ethnographic authority' to describe the way in which the author of the text constructs their own authority in order to convince the reader of the validity of their words (Rosaldo 1986: 78). Ethnographic authority, for the contemporary fieldworker, ultimately boils down to the statement 'I was there'. The ethnographer presents him or herself as the authority on a particular people because of the fieldwork experience that they undertake. In some ways this is related to Wagner's notion of embarrassment: 'I went through this process of struggle and hardship, I had to learn again from scratch what it meant to be a human being within this society, therefore I am the person to tell you what it was like.' As with Malinowski, it is a process of providing local colour and a convincing account: Malinowski begins his book *Argonauts of the Western Pacific* with a wonderful and evocative account of his arrival on the tropical beach of the Trobriand Islands, 'setting the scene' for his analysis and letting the reader know that he was there (1922: 1–6).

Finally, it can be the level of analysis that establishes the authority, even irrespective of the ethnographic details that support it: Evans-Pritchard does this in *Nuer Religion*, where he clearly rejects those parts of the fieldwork experience that do not support his theory, such as the meal that followed every sacrifice (1956). Whatever literary techniques are used, however, it is ultimately the plausibility of the author, their ability to convince the reader that they were there, as a trained ethnographer, that they observed the 'reality' of what was happening, and that they have been able to apply this reality to a wider theoretical context, that forms the basis for ethnographic authority (Geertz 1988). Once again, we have only the word of the ethnographer to persuade us, and their own literary ability to convince us. The final text is, inevitably, a highly subjective account.

Should this emphasis on subjectivity worry us? Eventually anthropology, and ethnography in general, came to the conclusion that it should not (Denzin 1997). Some ethnographers, or some accounts of how to do ethnography, point to processes such as 'grounded theory' or 'triangulation' that enable all elements of the work to be tested by reference to other sources, and so to be less reliant on the ethnographer (Strauss and Corbin 1990). Others make a virtue of ethnographic subjectivity and claim that so long as we know that the ethnographer comes with certain assumptions and presuppositions, is male or female, well educated, white, or whatever, then we can accept this as a partial view valid on its own terms, rather than a fully objective account of 'truth' (Hastrup 1995, Davies 1999). Others have tried to allow the voices of the people being studied to be heard alongside that of the ethnographer, to construct a multi-vocal text in which different perspectives are presented alongside each other, so allowing for a range of subjectivities that, it is hoped, may move towards a broader and more objective account (Denzin 1997). Whatever technique is used, the question of subjectivity and the personal involvement of the ethnographer can never be dismissed in contemporary anthropology. And that leads on to the next topic, which is the question of ethics.

## On Ethics

Reference to Malinowski's diaries also alerts us to some of the most significant ethical questions related to ethnography. Unlike textual study or philosophical enquiry, ethnographic fieldwork inevitably involves relations with other people, and so raises innumerable ethical issues. Malinowski's diaries draw our attention to two of these almost immediately. The first is the way in which the ethnographer treats the people being studied at a basic interpersonal level. It is very clear that much of Malinowski's behaviour at this level would be considered utterly inappropriate today, although that does not mean that some questionable behaviour does not still take place in the context of ethnography. The other, more philosophically significant, ethical questions relate to Malinowski's right to be studying the Trobriand Islanders in the first place and, ultimately, his right to speak on their behalf; to present their 'culture' to the world (Pratt 1986).

If we take the first of these ethical issues first, then, as already mentioned, many of the unsavoury practices of a Malinowksi, or even an Evans-Pritchard, would not be acceptable today (Meskell and Pels 2005). However, this does not negate the question. Wherever individuals are involved in some form of interaction with each other, particularly where 'power' is involved, then the abuse of power and the betrayal of that relationship is possible and the ethnographer is always prone to ethical dilemmas (Punch 1986). One significant context where this may happen is in gaining data under false pretences. It was common at one time for the ethnographer not to be concerned about telling the people being studied why he or she was there. There are stories of anthropologists telling their informants that they are studying 'history' or 'folklore' or some such topic, when really they are interested in the most intimate facts of the community's life. 'Covert ethnography' is generally frowned upon today except in very specific contexts, but the temptation to be a little flexible with the rationale or aims of the study remains (Punch 1986, 38–44). This is, I would always suggest, something to be avoided.

However, even if the ethnographer is candid about what they are doing and what they plan to do with the data that they collect, the pitfalls of interpersonal ethics remain. From collecting data for money, or drink, or some other favour, through to intimate and sexual relations with the informants, it matters that ethnographers are dealing with people (Kulick and Willson 1995). All ethnography is, at one level, exploitation. The ethnographer is asking something of the people being studied that is going to help his or her career, and can offer very little to the people in return. Being a university-educated academic, usually articulate, invariably confident and esentially in control, gives the ethnographer considerable power in most societies – where this is not the case, it is often identified in the text as exceptional (Punch 1986, 49–70). Having a tape recorder and a camera and other relevant technical equipment, or the trappings of wealth, may also place the ethnographer in a position of inequality in relation to the people being studied. These relationships need to be handled with care and respect, especially as the long-term nature of ethnography means that it is inevitable, over time, that one or more of the people being studied will really annoy the ethnographer and lead to some form of unthinking behaviour.

Of course, the problems and questions may not all be one way. It is inevitable that the community under consideration, and certain members of that community in particular, will manipulate or exploit the ethnographer for their own purposes. This may be part of a local power struggle. It may be for economic gain, for wider political purposes, or for other less tangible reasons. The ethnographer is the outsider in the context of the community. The ethnographer is, at least at the beginning of the fieldwork, the person with least knowledge of how the community works, and the particular power struggles and internal tensions that it contains (Boissevain 1980). The ethnographer, therefore, is wide open to exploitation by those who wish to take advantage of their presence. None of this may be considered 'right' in any ethical sense, but it is arguable that being caught up in such games is not in itself an 'ethical failure' on the part of the ethnographer, unless he or she chooses to get involved in a way that harms the community for their own academic purposes (Pearson 2002).

The second question I raised at the beginning of this section, however, is by far the more interesting and potentially the most disturbing. What right does the ethnographer have to be doing fieldwork in the first place, and what right does he or she have to speak on behalf of the community, or to present their life and culture in a way that they may not have approved? This issue goes right to the heart of ethnography.

Anthropology no longer adopts the world view expressed by Beattie, in which the primary purpose of the discipline is to 'collect' and 'record' all the cultures of the world before they disappear (Beattie 1964). The very idea that there are a finite number of cultures to be collected is open to debate as culture changes, merges and transforms itself continually in all parts of the world. What, therefore, does contemporary anthropology see as its academic purpose? There are probably two kinds of answer, which also address the ethical question of the ethnographer's right to tell the story of the society being studied. The first focuses on the subject of the study. Ethnography is undertaken on behalf of communities or societies with a specific problem that they wish to address, believing that a detailed in-depth study of their community or organization will help. Here the motivation for the study often comes from the community being studied and the ethnographer is, more or less, their employee (Wulff and Fiske 1987). Of course there are variations on this theme and the community may be just one of the parties involved in the initiation of the project, but all these types of ethnographic project fall into the same category. The second approach sees the purpose of anthropology as being what it has always been, the greater knowledge and understanding of humanity in all its diverse forms, and the purpose of ethnography is seen as the furtherance of that wider knowledge.

Ethically the first of these purposes offers fewer difficulties, although we come back again to the question of interpersonal relations and power structures, especially where the ethnographer is in the pay of the community or organization that has initiated a study of itself (Punch 1986: 49–70). These issues, however, do not relate directly to the wider question of 'purpose' or 'rights' as outlined above. It is with the second form of purpose that the question of 'rights' really comes into its own. We can identify the need to understand as much as possible about the way humans function in society, their interactions, kinship systems,

languages, political behaviour, economic relations, processes of production or whatever it might be that we wish to study. The real question
is how this justifies the ethnographer turning up out of the blue within
a community that cannot really choose whether to accept their presence among them or not, and then writing a text which the people
may never be able to read, let alone respond to. The primary way
through this quandary for today's anthropologists has been to engage
the community actively in the process of study and to make the process
a cooperative one which brings both some benefits to the community
and also enables the ethnographer to draw out, and publish, wider
theoretical issues (Lassiter 2005, Denzin 1997). That is the situation
that has obtained in all the studies that are drawn on for this book.

All the studies that underpin this text have been undertaken primarily for the benefit of those being studied (in one way or another)
and for the secondary purpose of gaining an academic qualification for
the researcher involved. It is only subsequent to this initial purpose on
the part of the primary ethnographers that I, as an anthropologist and
coordinator of the project, have drawn on their work (with their
permission but not, I have to say, with the explicit permission of the
subjects of each individual study) to say something more about the
nature of religion. Maintaining a degree of anonymity on behalf of the
communities studied, and the intention not to identify any individuals
within these communities, has helped this more abstract purpose, but
the baseline remains: I am drawing on the words and images of
ordinary people observed going about their ordinary business
throughout England, in order to make a serious theoretical statement
about the nature of religion. This leads me to an account of how the
material that makes up this study was produced.


## The Worship in Birmingham Project

On completion of my PhD thesis I knew that I wanted to continue in
some way to use ethnography in order to understand more about what
I would then have called 'mainstream English religion', that is the
religious life of the principal Christian churches. I did not, however,
pursue this directly. My first job was as a church-based community

worker employed by the Anglican Church in Manchester to help a group of thirteen inner-city churches to respond to the needs of young families in the area. My ethnographic experience proved very useful in this context, and it was always clear that one element of the post was to conduct research among the churches and people of the inner city. I was employed for five years and worked with many different groups in the city, and the long-term nature of this work, along with my 'participant observer' status, meant that this was an ideal setting for ethnographic study. I was not, however, primarily involved in research although I maintained field notes and wrote some reports for the project. I would not count this as real ethnographic experience.

It was in this context, however, that some of the ideas that form the basis for the following chapters began to emerge. I was not only talking to people who were members of the churches, I was also attending, on a regular basis, parent and toddler groups and other meetings where young families gathered. I was listening to a wide cross-section of the people of the inner city in a framework where religion and religious ideas were central. I was in many ways in a privileged situation. I was not ordained, but I was known to be working for the church. As I talked and listened to people they soon became aware that I was not going to offer the kind of condemnation of their religious practices that they assumed they would receive from ordained ministers. They found in me a willing ear to listen to the many stories they had of contact with astrology, spiritualism, fortune-tellers, local healers of one sort or another, and so on. All this material was noted and has continued to puzzle me as I moved on to other places and other activities.

What is more, it was clear that it was not just the people outside, or on the edge of the church, who talked about and engaged with these alternative forms of religious practice. It soon became clear, through meeting members of congregations in many different contexts, not all of which were church-based, that many ordinary members of the various Christian congregations also followed these practices, and this more than anything else confirmed for me the value of the long-term, slow but steady ethnography I was engaged in. By gaining the trust of church members, meeting people in many different circumstances, being prepared to listen when nobody else would, I was learning things about these people and their lives that the clergy, and many of their friends within the congregations, simply did not know. I was moving below the surface to something deeper and far more intimate within their lives. That intimacy of understanding, I would argue, is what ethnography has to offer.

Ethnography, however, is always limited, as already mentioned, by being local and specific. After five years I knew a great deal about the religious lives of young mothers within a very small area of East Manchester in the mid-1980s. I cannot really claim that this has any significance for others in other situations and other times. The only way in which we can begin to generalize from one context of ethnography is through comparative studies, where a significant number of individual studies of many different contexts are undertaken, to enable a viable comparison to be made. There was no way, however, that I could begin to undertake enough individual studies on my own to be able to provide the data needed for serious comparative analysis.

From Manchester I was lucky enough to obtain a post as a lecturer in the sociology and anthropology of religion at Birmingham University, and it was on a departmental visit to Chicago that a possible answer to my concerns about ethnography emerged. In Chicago I met Lowell Livezey from the University of Illinois, director of the Religion in Urban America Project (Livezey 2000). This was a Lilly Foundation-funded project that aimed to study a series of neighbourhoods within the Chicago area through specific ethnographic research in each locality. Teams of ethnographers were brought together to undertake their fieldwork simultaneously, each project being expected to provide a detailed exploration of the religious life of their own neighbourhood, and the comparative study of these separate ethnographies would provide the overall findings of the Project. Here was a Project that focused on religion, which combined the best of ethnographic work with a comparative method that aimed at overcoming one of its most serious drawbacks. Here was something I could perhaps try to recreate in Birmingham.

Unfortunately, however, there are no major trusts in Britain equivalent to the Lilly Foundation who would fund a project on the scale of the Religion in Urban America Project. I therefore had to explore different possibilities for generating a team of ethnographers. Fortunately, the following year I had a series of six independent requests from potential postgraduate research students to study different aspects of life in religious communities in Birmingham or the surrounding area. Each student had a specific purpose for their research, but each student was also open to the possibility of using ethnographic methods in order to explore their chosen topic. In order to draw these diverse student projects together I invented the title of 'The Worship in Birmingham Project', and held regular seminars and annual conferences for the students involved and for others interested in similar themes (Stringer 2002).

The title, however, proved unhelpful. I had intended to follow through my previous work on worship, but very few of the students I attracted were particularly interested in worship. I had also assumed that most students would be working in Birmingham or its environs but, while that was the case technically, the most significant projects were based some distance from Birmingham, as far apart as Liverpool and the edge of the Norfolk Broads. This, however, did not matter to the Project since the material that was being collected was of very high quality and has, as this book tries to show, led to some very exciting comparative work. In fact, the various individual projects within the wider Project related much more directly to the work I had been doing in East Manchester among the young mothers of the inner city than it ever did to the themes of my PhD. It is the wider question of religious practice among ordinary members of congregations, and those on the edge or beyond the church, therefore, that has formed the basis for this comparative analysis.

The only factor, therefore, that really links the various studies that come together to inform this work is that they were conducted through the methodology of ethnography, with all the advantages and disadvantages that this offers. The vast majority were conducted under my supervision, although I am not sure that this has provided any real unity. What was more important, however, was that the students involved came together on a regular basis to share their ideas, their findings and their problems and it is that team effort, with a community of scholars working on different projects but with considerable interaction between them, that I think has been one of the most significant features of this work. This has also led, I would like to think, to the other major common factor that I have noted among the students involved. All of them have commented that the ethnographic methods they used have led directly to results and conclusions they had never expected. Most students came to their project with a specific question that they wished to ask. Most discovered, through spending considerable lengths of time listening carefully to the people involved in their study, that other issues were far more important to the people than those they had wanted to study, and this led most of them to change the direction of their study at some point during their work. The specific factors that were of more importance could generally be classed as local and personal religious practices of a sort that surprised the ethnographer, and it was this entirely unexpected finding that forms the basis for this book and the arguments that it contains. Without ethnography, what I am presenting in this text would never have been discovered.

## The Structure of the Argument

Over the next three chapters, therefore, I wish to present a range of material drawn from the different studies that I undertook in Manchester, or that my students have been involved in, over the past ten years. I want, in each of the following three chapters, to address one of the three bases for the definition of religion that I raised in Chapter One. In Chapter Three I shall consider the unity of religion through a discussion of belief. In Chapter Four I shall focus on sacred space and tackle the question of transcendence in religion. In Chapter Five I shall discuss attitudes to 'narratives of the non-empirical' based primarily on the work that I undertook with the young mothers in Manchester.

In Chapter Six I want to raise the question of gender. Almost all the people I or my students have talked and listened to during our studies have been women, mostly working-class women. The question that must be addressed, therefore, is whether the model of religion that we have been observing, and that I am trying to highlight in this text, is a specifically gendered model or one that has a significant class bias. Chapter Six will address these issues, and also return to the questions of subjectivity and ethics in ethnography that have been raised in this chapter.

Finally, Chapter Seven will return to the questions of my opening chapter, and ask whether we are in a position to present a new definition of religion – a definition not based on Christian or previous Western academic models.

# Chapter Three

# Of Requiems and Reincarnation

About two weeks before setting out for China in the autumn of 2003, where I was to present some preliminary thoughts on the ideas contained in this book, one of my students turned up in my office – very, very angry. He is a priest in the Church of England who ministers to a socially deprived area of Birmingham. He came to me originally because he wanted to explore how his church could reach out to a community where the majority of men were unemployed, crime and vandalism were high, and most parents were unmarried. He knew that nearly all the young mothers of the neighbourhood came to his church when their children were born to ask for them to be baptized. The mothers, however, never came to worship. He had laid on educational programmes to teach the mothers what Christian baptism meant and what the church could do for them. And, despite his insisting that all mothers who wanted their children baptized come to these classes, neither the mothers nor their children ever started coming to worship.

The priest had thought that the problem lay primarily with the church, that it was simply not 'getting its message across' appropriately to this particular population, so he came to me to undertake a PhD which would help him listen to the young mothers of the area, and perhaps enable him to communicate the Gospel to them. Unfortunately, however, the project was never completed due to family and work pressures on the priest.

In 2003, as a student, he had been working with me for about two years, doing ethnographic fieldwork elsewhere in the city, in an area similar to his own community. He had found places where the young mothers met and turned up to listen to their conversations, getting to know them, building up their trust and trying to see life from their point of view.

One day, he suddenly burst into my office. He explained that once he heard what the women were saying, he was both shocked and angry – shocked because he realized that they fully understood the priestly message he had been teaching, but felt that it had nothing to do with them or their desire for their children's baptism; and angry because he could not make these women see the inconsistencies of their own thinking. When talking about their own children, they said that they had to be baptized in order to go to heaven when they died. Baptism was essential for the future benefit of the children, and the women would see themselves as very bad mothers if they did not do this for their child. When asked about other people who had never been baptized, or about heaven and hell, then the same women were adamant that every single person was going to heaven because they could not believe in a God who would send people to hell. So, my student asked, if every person is going to heaven anyway, why do you need to get your child baptized in order to ensure that he or she will go to heaven? This was plainly illogical. He could see it, the women could see it, but it did not matter. It was still essential for these women that they got their children baptized, because this would ensure that they would go to heaven.

There are other contexts where contradictory religious views were identified. In a Manchester church where I worked we held an open discussion on death. I did not engage in the discussion, but simply listened and let the members of the congregation discuss the issues in their own way. It was an Anglo-Catholic church and the conversation began by stating the usual Catholic position that when a relative dies it is important to say a requiem mass, and to pray for the soul of the person who has died, in order to ensure that they will get to heaven. There was no surprise here: it is the belief we would have expected. Suddenly, however, in the middle of this predictable conversation, one of those present happened to say that they liked the idea of reincarnation, the idea that when a person dies their soul returns to earth in a new body – an idea that is totally at odds with Christian thinking. Once the idea had been raised, however, practically everybody in the room, all of whom were regular churchgoers, claimed that they also believed they would be reincarnated rather than going to heaven. This did not appear to negate the importance of praying for the dead or the idea that their relatives would go to heaven; reincarnation was what the members of the group wanted for themselves. It was abundantly clear that two, totally contradictory, beliefs were being held, consciously and adamantly, by each person.

When I, or my students, listened to what people said in many different contexts, we discovered that contradictory beliefs were not unusual, although the two examples above may be seen as extreme cases. People may hold any number of totally contradictory beliefs, and use them in different circumstances for different purposes. So, for example, it is believed to be essential that we do all we can to help those closest to us, particularly in relation to death. If that means baptizing our children or praying for the souls of our dead relatives, then that is what we will do. When it comes to other people, however, people unrelated to us, then it does not really matter: we can think more widely and believe that God must be good and will allow everybody into heaven anyway. When it comes to ourselves, on the other hand, heaven does not sound such an exciting place, but as rather dull and boring, and we would prefer to have another life here on earth, so the concept of reincarnation sounds more reassuring. Of course many other beliefs are also held alongside these, and, in relation to death and the dead in particular, such beliefs appear to multiply enormously. Before considering death, however, which I will do in subsequent chapters, we need to look more closely at the notion of 'belief'.

## Belief

Belief is an essentially Christian concept. Other religions are based primarily on 'doing': following the law, performing ritual, and so on. This does not mean that other religions do not have a concept of belief (although this is debatable). It means that for them belief, if it is relevant, is secondary to other elements of the religion. For Christianity, by contrast, belief is central. Early Christians were distinguished by the fact that they 'believed' that Jesus was the Son of God. This notion was later clarified and codified in relation to Greek philosophy and led both to the great heresy debates of the third and fourth centuries, and to the 'creeds' which became central to Christian ritual. The emphasis on belief was reinforced during the Reformation, with its emphasis on 'justification by faith', and from this time on, even in the Western intellectual tradition, Christianity has always been associated with belief. The Enlightenment led to the 'privatization' of religion, which was seen to be based on the beliefs of the individual, and the prevailing rationalism led to the rejection of religion on the basis of a rejection of 'belief': specifically beliefs that were defined as 'irrational'. During the nineteenth century, this emphasis on belief was also applied to other religious traditions through the work of Max Müller and others (Sugirtharaja 2003). Edward Tylor, for example, as we have seen in Chapter One, defined 'religion' as the 'belief in Spiritual Beings' (1871: I, 383). While many people questioned whether religion should be defined in relation to 'spiritual beings', nobody seemed to question whether the application of the concept of 'belief' to other religions was relevant or even possible (Stringer 1999b).

Belief, therefore, is an issue that anthropologists have, on the whole, been very reluctant to tackle. Robertson Smith (1894) argued that what people say about their rituals should be secondary to what they actually do. Beliefs, he claimed, change over time and are often created 'post-hoc', whereas the ritual generally remains static. This has led anthropologists to apply most of their attention to what is 'done' during religious ritual, rather than what believers say about it. There has, it is true, always been a strong interest in 'myth' within anthropology, but this is not synonymous with 'belief' even if, for many commentators, myth appears to imply some kind of belief. The debate about the relationship between myth and ritual has tended, on the whole, to ignore the relationship of belief with these separate concepts.

A more recent tendency in anthropology has been the attempt to construct a system of beliefs – not unlike systematic Christian theology – that is both coherent and all-embracing. E. E. Evans-Pritchard's *Nuer Religion* is important in this respect, in taking what the people 'believe' seriously for the first time in anthropology (1956). However, as I suggested in Chapter One, this book may be more a reflection of Evans-Pritchard's own systematic imagination, strongly influenced by his recent conversion to Catholicism, than a reflection of the actual 'beliefs' of the Nuer themselves.

More recently the concept of 'belief' and related notions have been subject to more detailed criticism, and the wider debate about the meaning of specific words has become a field open for study. For example, Jean Poullion tackles the issue of belief in other societies by asking whether those who do not share our language do in fact 'believe' in the way that is implied when we use the term (1982). This leads Poullion to look at the term and to distinguish its meanings, in French, so that he can look more closely at what the French, and people of other language groups, might be saying when they use the term. Poullion is keen to point out that it is usually European anthropologists who claim that other people 'believe', not the people themselves. This, he argues, is a direct result of the nature of the verb 'to believe'.

Poullion distinguishes three uses of the French verb 'croire' (2). These three uses are best translated into English as 'to trust in', 'to believe that' and 'to believe in'. At the root of this distinction is the assumption, made explicit by Poullion, that if we say that we 'believe' a particular statement, then there must be some doubt concerning the truth of that statement. If we say, for example, that we 'believe' in God, then the statement about God, the concept of 'God', must be open to question. This sense of doubt, Poullion argues, is central to the European understanding of the verb 'to believe'. Without that doubt, we simply 'believe that … ', or we could say that we 'know that … ': we know that our friend exists, we know that stones fall, or whatever. Other languages, Poullion argues, do not necessarily have this distinction, or they make it explicit by the use of distinct terms. Pouillon claims that it is the very ambiguity of the term 'to believe' that gives it its usefulness and power in European languages. This ambiguity, however, does not necessarily translate into other languages around the world.

Martin Southwold picks up a very similar point in his own discussion of belief among the village Buddhists he studied in Sri Lanka (1983: 150f.). For Southwold, it is the distinction between 'belief that' and 'belief in' that is the vital one, and he expresses this in relation to Christian theology and especially arguments about the existence of God. To say we 'believe that God exists' is to make a statement similar to saying that we know a table, or a friend, exists. Such a statement would, therefore, invite a discussion of its truth. However, for Southwold this is only half the story. He argues that the understanding of the word 'exists' in both these statements is acknowledged to be different, because 'God' is a different kind of term from 'table' or 'friend'. More importantly, however, Southwold claims that we very rarely hear people make a statement to the effect that they 'believe that' God exists; rather they are more likely to say, as the Christian creeds do, that they 'believe in' God. To 'believe in' God is, as with Pouillon, to put one's trust in God, to have faith in God, not to make any special reference to God's existence or to the nature of that existence. To believe in God is to take God as an assumption, a starting point, and to move forward from that point.

## Belief statements

Throughout his work Southwold chooses to use the more specific term 'belief statements' rather than the more vague 'beliefs'. In doing so, he makes comments about the village Buddhists among whom he is working which are similar to those I made at the start of this chapter. The village Buddhists, it appears, use specific statements of belief in everyday conversations, sometimes at cross-purposes, but with an implied sense of a wider system behind them. However, Southwold makes a distinction between 'belief statements' and 'symbolic state-ments' (50) on the basis of the kind of truth that is being assumed (whether empirical or metaphorical). It is this distinction I would like to question.

In order to do this I need to turn to the work of Dan Sperber (1974, 1982). Sperber does not deal with 'belief' as such, but rather with symbols, or what he prefers to call 'symbolic statements' (1974: 3). He claims that 'symbols do not mean' (85f.), a statement which seems to contradict the concensus of anthropological thought on the subject of symbolism, the main aim of which has been to discover meanings. He begins his argument by criticizing Victor Turner and other anthro-pologists for taking too much notice of what people say about the meaning of their symbols. Sperber suggests that any such 'native exegesis' of the symbol should itself be treated as an extension of that symbol, which consequently requires an explanation in its own right. In other words, when the Ndembu tell us that the *mudyi* tree stands for mother's milk or the matrilineal clan during female initiation rites (Turner 1967: 20–25), or when Roman Catholics talk about 'transubstantiation' and claim that the bread at the eucharist becomes the body of Christ, this cannot in any way help us explain what the rite in question 'means'. Such statements can only take the problem one stage further, in the sense that the statement itself, the relationship between a symbol and its meaning, demands an explanation.

Sperber goes on to draw a distinction between different kinds of 'truth' in his analysis. He claims that certain statements – the example he uses from his own fieldwork is 'all leopards are Christians' – do not need to be empirically 'true', although they may be treated as such by the people concerned. For these people, therefore, when they affirm the 'truth' of the statement, what is 'true' is the related statement that '"all leopards are Christians" is true'. This may sound a rather pedantic distinction, but once we grasp what Sperber is saying, I think it will prove useful. The point at issue is not the empirical truth of the statement itself, but the fact that people are willing to accept such a statement as 'true' without questioning its empirical truth. This is what Sperber calls 'putting the statement in parenthesis', setting it apart from ordinary discourse. It is only 'true' because it is said to be 'true' although the exact nature of that 'truth' should not be, and on the whole is not, questioned (1974: 91f.). What is more, this construction of truth in parenthesis allows for a multiplicity of statements to be held at any one time, even if logically speaking they are mutually contradictory (94–5).

The same can be said for much of the religious discourse of any Christian church. All the doctrines of such a church are 'true' only in this Sperberian sense. Where I differ from Sperber, however, is over the 'empirical truth' of such a statement. Sperber takes it for granted that statements like 'all leopards are Christians' or 'the bread is the body of Christ' are quite obviously untrue. That, according to him, is how we can distinguish a symbolic statement in the first place (2–3). It is not clear to me how he can be so sure of this. It is only within a certain Western 'scientific' discourse, one that defines the word 'empirical' as Sperber is using it, that such statements have no truth. There is, however, by all known methods of proof, no way of knowing whether leopards are Christians or whether the bread in the Eucharist is the body of Christ. What Sperber should be saying is that the 'empirical truth' of such statements does not matter, that this is not an issue that anybody would normally dream of raising, that the question is irrelevant. For the ordinary member of the society that Sperber studied, and for the ordinary Catholic, the truth of such statements is simply taken for granted.

## The Question of Proof

During a seminar I once presented on my study of a Roman Catholic congregation (Stringer 1999a: 109–37), I was asked how far the Mass 'proved' the existence of God. This struck me at the time as a very strange question. The implication behind it was that normal, rational people could not accept such nonsensical notions as the existence of God and what is more, that only those who go to Mass hold such strange, irrational beliefs. Somehow, therefore, what goes on during the Mass must 'prove' that God exists if it is to persuade otherwise rational people to accept such irrational ideas. That, however, presents completely the wrong picture and, I would suggest, begins from the wrong end of the argument.

This is best illustrated by a short passage from Southwold's book in which he talks about the creation story in Genesis (1983: 76). Southwold comments that this story, whether taken literally or not, is usually seen as saying something about God, about God's creativity, God's love, or – at the extreme, and following one line of argument – about God's very existence. Southwold suggests that this is not the point of the story at all. If we expect such stories to tell us about God, then we are looking at them from the wrong angle. 'God' in such stories, Southwold argues, should be taken as a basic assumption, an unquestioned 'truth', as should God's goodness, God's love, and so on. What the story is saying, according to Southwold, is that *if* God is 'good', which we accept without question, and *if* God created the world, as the story tells us, then the world itself must be good. It is the assumptions that we make about God that give significance to the world, and not the other way around.

Southwold goes on to say much the same about the doctrine of the incarnation, namely that it is not an erudite philosophical argument about the nature of God, but rather that if God, whom we know to be good, takes on human form, then humanity must in consequence be 'blessed', be special, or even be divine. The discourse is not one about the nature of God but one about the world, about humanity, about ourselves and our everyday lives, one which takes the existence and nature of God as a given.

Much the same, therefore, can be said about the Mass, but in a rather more complex fashion. The Mass can no more prove the existence of God than can the first four chapters of Genesis. The Mass is played out within a framework of what Southwold would call belief statements, the truth of which is not to be questioned. It is these statements, therefore, fervently held and known to be 'true', that give significance to the Mass. The Mass cannot prove that the bread becomes the body of Christ, but the knowledge of that 'truth' – the statement held in parenthesis, as Sperber would put it – gives the Mass its significance; by implication it also gives anything else that is brought into that Mass, from the individual's personal life or elsewhere, the same kind of significance.

The questions still remain, however, where the source of these basic true statements is to be found, and why people are so willing, in fact eager, to hold them as 'true' despite an environment beyond, and sometimes within, the church that claims, like Sperber, that they must be false. As Sperber says in a different context, the acceptance of the explanation must itself be explained.

In an article titled 'Is symbolic thought prerational?' (1982), Sperber develops some of his ideas on symbolism one step further. He re-emphasizes the point that symbols do not 'mean', and claims that they can help us to manipulate ideas that the rational part of our brain cannot cope with. The question that Sperber asks is: if symbols do not 'mean', in the normal sense of the word, then what is it that they do?

For Sperber, what symbols do is to 'evoke', but he is never entirely clear what it is that is being evoked. At one level what is being evoked is purely an emotional response that has no rational basis. At another level it is some kind of interconnection between ideas such that the idea of bread, for example, will always be related to the concept of the body of Christ. Sperber, however, rejects both these suggestions as too simplistic, and claims that what is evoked is neither an emotion nor a connection of ideas, but rather a system of thought in which the associations that are presented do in fact make sense. In other words bread does not in itself evoke the idea of Jesus' body, or anything else; rather, the quotation 'bread equals body' evokes the system of thought in which this equation makes sense, that is, the whole tradition of the Roman Catholic Church.

If we acknowledge this argument and substitute the idea of a 'belief statement' for what Sperber calls a 'symbolic statement', then we could say that a belief statement is a statement that is set apart from ordinary discourse, one whose truth is not questioned at an empirical level and which evokes a system of thought within which that statement makes sense. This would match nicely with Pouillon's understanding of belief as implying at least some kind of doubt. The belief statement is of a different order from ordinary discourse. It is a symbolic statement whose empirical truth is irrelevant, a statement that evokes a system of thought, a total system of belief, very like the one that Evans-Pritchard constructed for the Nuer, a system within which such statements do, in fact, make sense.

Here, however, I would claim that the argument begins to fall apart. Sperber's argument may well be correct for Roman Catholics, who have a clear and structured system of theology, though this assumption might also be questioned. For the Anglicans of my original example or the women wanting their children baptized, however, I would want to question Sperber's assumptions and look much more closely at the disjointed nature of the belief statements being used, their total lack of reference to belief systems, and the seeming inconsistency of these belief statements in relation to death.

## The Sociology of Superstition

Sociologists have, on the whole, been much more willing than anthropologists to acknowledge the place of belief within their studies. This is probably because they are working within their own society, where beliefs do tend to have an importance that is not so obvious or so easily noticeable in other societies. During the 1970s a number of researchers went out and spent some time living in different parts of

Britain, usually in fairly isolated communities, and asked questions about the role of religion within these communities (Moore 1974; Clark 1982). The emphasis in these studies was primarily on social factors associated with religious belonging rather than belief as such, but the studies did provide some ideas and data that can be compared with my own research and that of my students.

One typical example was David Clark's study of a North Yorkshire fishing village, *Under Pulpit and Pew* (1982). The community in question was almost entirely Methodist or Congregational in its church attendance, with a small Roman Catholic presence and a very marginal Anglican church. As the study progresses we learn a great deal about the community, the views of its members, the organization of the chapels and the rivalry between them. Belief, however, is never really explored beyond saying that, like everything else in the village, it is 'old-fashioned'.

The premise that Clark is working on is that there is a fundamental conflict between 'official' belief and what is variously termed 'folk' belief, 'popular' belief, or 'superstition' (7f.). It is clear to Clark that there must be a distinction between these two types of belief, as it is said to be clear to the leaders of the various churches and chapels. How clear this distinction is to the average member of the congregations, however, or even to the ordinary villagers, is more debatable. Clark gives an excellent analysis of the history of the area, showing how the old superstitious beliefs of the fishermen was hardly touched by Christianity until the Methodist preachers arrived in the late eighteenth century. From that time on, however, while there was a constant tension between superstition and official belief in the eyes of the religious establishment, the people themselves seem to have kept the two very much apart: the official beliefs are for the chapel, the superstitions are for the shoreline. This all seems to make a great deal of sense.

However, I would question the real nature of the distinction that Clark draws between 'official' and 'popular' beliefs. Clark is seeing the village mainly from the point of view of the official religion – he even acknowledges this at times – and not as one of the villagers. How far, therefore, do the people themselves see these two forms of 'belief' as being in conflict? There is, I would suggest, enough evidence even in

Clark's own study to raise the question and, I think, to offer an alternative answer.

A similar question could be raised for the members of the congregations of the churches whom I and my students have studied, and those on the edges of these congregations. As I sat listening to conversations in Manchester at various times when some matter of belief was being discussed, I felt the usefulness of Clark's distinction between official and popular belief. There were a number of women at one parent and toddler group, for example, who firmly believed in the power of astrology and in the healing powers of spiritualist healers, even though neither was part of official 'church' doctrine. These were, in the church's view, 'superstitions'. I was, of course, aware of the 'official' doctrine and I knew that what was being talked about here was not in line with that teaching. But does this mean that for the people themselves there were two clearly distinct sets of beliefs? I would argue not.

The article that follows Pouillon's discussion of belief in the same book is Nicole Belmont's 'Superstition and popular religion in Western societies' (1982). In this paper, Belmont argues for a distinction between superstition or popular beliefs, and official beliefs, similar to that which Clark was developing. She goes on to suggest that this must always be true where the Christian religion is dominant, because the very systematic approach to belief of Christianity makes it impossible to take account of every aspect of an individual's life. Belmont argues, therefore, that there are large areas of life that Christianity fails to touch (including those dealing with sickness, danger or uncertainty), leaving the potential for the continuation of pagan practices as 'superstitions'. This is almost exactly what Clark was arguing in relation to his fishing village, and the same could also be said of the women at the parent and toddler group and their astrology (as we shall see in Chapter Five). As long as Christianity fails to take the real dangers of the fishing industry or the problems of inner-city poverty seriously, superstitions or popular beliefs relating to these dangers will continue.

This argument is very persuasive within a historical overview, and as such I would probably want to agree with it. Where I would want to question it, however, is in the way that such issues are viewed from the point of view of the ordinary people involved. All the views that draw a distinction between official and popular belief – Clark's, those of the clergy in mainline churches, Belmont's, even my own preconceived ideas – are looking at the situation from the top down. What would the same situation look like if viewed from the bottom up? Would it be any different?

Geoffrey Ahern's contribution to the book *Inner City God,* "'I do believe in Christmas": white working-class people and Anglican clergy in inner-city London' (1987), suggests what a bottom-up view might look like. This work is based on a 'qualitative survey', that is on long interviews with specific individuals in the East End of London. The people interviewed had no specific links with the churches, and therefore Ahern was able to investigate how ordinary non-churchgoers understood their beliefs. The survey draws out a number of points, including the 'them and us' attitude to the church, the fact that people's beliefs were clearly dependent on their past, and how difficult people appeared to find it to talk about specific beliefs at all. None of these conclusions in themselves are very remarkable. If we take these points in reverse order, however, we can see something very similar to the kind of argument that I have been developing in this chapter.

First, we are told that ordinary people cannot fully articulate their beliefs. This is very common and, following Southwold's argument, should not surprise us. Beliefs are simply there. They are accepted as true and never questioned. What Ahern's survey does show, however, is that beliefs can exist in many different forms: as stories and images, as well as in the form of specific statements. Secondly, therefore, Ahern argues that beliefs and belief statements are related to past experiences. Again this appears to be obvious once we think about it. Ahern talks of elderly men who had been in the trenches during the First World War, and of how their most fundamental assertions related directly to this experience and were expressed in relation to stories about it.

Any body of ideas about the world that an individual has, any series of 'belief statements', will grow over time. They will relate to significant times in that person's life. It is this very process of growing, however, which means that, for most people, these statements will exist largely in isolation from each other, each one related to a particular event in the past, but they are never seen as a whole or as related to each other.

Here again we see that it is impossible for people to articulate their beliefs, not simply because they have not formulated them, but also because they have never previously been asked to connect them within a single discourse.

This brings us to the 'them and us' attitude to the church. As we have seen, a system of beliefs is itself a central belief within most Christian contexts. This is seen far more clearly by those outside the church than by those inside. What is more, those outside also appear to see the contradictions and confusions in the way individuals relate to particular belief statements from within the system, and often therefore dismiss church people as 'hypocrites' (Stringer 2004). Those outside the churches, however, still need belief statements for themselves. They draw on any that are to hand or that have helped in the past, without being too concerned about their source or making any distinction between 'official beliefs' and 'superstitions'. They also reject those that are irrelevant or have harmed them in the past. Above all they do not fit these belief statements into any kind of 'framework', but simply draw on those that are relevant to the situation in hand.

## A Situational Theory of Belief

What implications does this have for our understanding of 'belief'? I will draw together the ideas that I have already presented in this chapter, and show how beliefs are held and used by ordinary people. The purpose of this argument is not to make sense of isolated examples, of particular statements of belief, but to create a complete picture to explain an individual's long-term behaviour: they may state one belief one day and another the next without realizing that the two are, by academic reckoning, mutually incompatible. This is not a matter of ignorance; there is clearly a deeper reason for it.

Earlier in the chapter I referred to Sperber's notion that belief statements are different kinds of statement from the ordinary, everyday views of a member of the church congregation. To say 'I believe' implies that what is 'believed' cannot be proved empirically and that the empirical truth of the statement is largely irrelevant; to say 'I believe' is to make a 'symbolic' assertion. Sperber assumes that what is asserted – or as he would put it, what is 'evoked' – by such a statement is a 'system' of beliefs. I see this as a distraction. What is important is not the system, but the individual statement made at a particular time for a particular purpose. If this is the case, then the distinction that has been made between superstition and official belief becomes irrelevant. A person, we are assuming, will state any belief, official or popular, that is of value to them at any particular moment and in any particular situation. From this I would argue – and the previous example of the discussion group in the Anglo-Catholic church would support this – that most ordinary Christians do not even think in terms of systematic beliefs or systems of theology; rather, they tend to think in terms of specific belief statements as and when these statements are needed (Stringer 1999a: 177–80).

What still needs to be asked, of course, is why we need such statements at all. Here I think we must return to Sperber, who argues (1982) that we use a symbolic statement when our minds cannot cope with the irrationality of the situation, when an empirical statement no longer makes sense. So belief statements are used to deal with illness, misfortune and grief; to express a sense of something beyond ourselves, something over which we have no control; to provide security; and to justify actions that are largely unjustifiable. In all these cases the assertion of 'belief' transfers the argument away from the everyday to the 'sacred', to the special, to the 'other'. Belief gives the argument a special power and relevance. This is as true for superstition as it is for official beliefs.

It is also at this point that we must move from Pouillon's 'belief that' to Southwold's 'belief in'. It is because belief statements are empirically unverifiable that we have to commit ourselves to them, to assert them as truth, and to trust them implicitly. It is this that gives them their emotional power and significance.

This is an argument I will come back to in Chapter Five. For now, what is important is to accept that for most ordinary people in England the idea of a coherent system of beliefs held by each individual is meaningless. For these people 'religion', whatever we might mean by it as an encounter with the non-empirical, is not systematic at all: for most people, 'religion' is situational and often contradictory. Why should this not be true of 'religion' in general?

Chapter Four

# Of Graveyards and Kitchens

In the previous chapter we looked at the concept of belief and, through an analysis of how belief statements are used in ordinary discourse, I suggested that coherence is not central to how many people in contemporary England understand religion. In this chapter I wish to consider the second area of concern that I raised in the introduction, the idea of 'transcendence'. I wish to show, as I did with 'coherence' in relation to belief, that the idea of transcendence is not central to most discourses about the non-empirical in English society. I wish to do this by looking at the concept of sacred space, and in particular at how such space is categorized as 'sacred'.

Space has clearly been an issue that has been developed in both the study of religion and in anthropology. However, in neither discipline has the understanding of space been theorized as much as we might assume (Low and Lawrence-Zúñiga 2003, Knott 2005). One example of this is the still common use of the term 'sacred space' without any real discussion of what it might mean. In contemporary geography the concepts of space and location have been explored in detail, and ideas of landscape, multilocality, contested spaces, embodied spaces, narrative spaces and spatial tactics are commonplace (Low and Lawrence-Zúñiga 2003). My object in this chapter, however, is not to discuss space and location as such, or even the interaction between the individual and 'sacred space'. I want to use a discussion of space to explore the idea of 'transcendence'. In doing this I will be touching on a number of issues mentioned earlier.

## The Space of the Sanctuary

I wish to begin with the most traditional example of 'sacred space' that emerged from the contexts studied in the Worship in Birmingham Project. One of my female students wanted to study the lives and attitudes of women in a traditional Anglo-Catholic church in central Birmingham (Schofield 1999). This was a few years after the authorization of women's ordination in the Anglican Church, and she was interested in why the women of this parish held such conservative views on this issue. She started with the clear hope of changing minds and helping the women to see what she understood as the contradictions in their position. She left the field, however, with a far deeper understanding of these women's point of view, and while going forward to ordination herself, she continued to admire their integrity and value what they had taught her. It is not, however, my student's wider project that concerns me in this chapter, but the story of one woman in particular.

The church was situated in a deprived inner-city neighbourhood with a strong multi-ethnic population. A local mosque was being built close by, and the area had suffered from a series of violent attacks involving gangs and guns. The women in the church were of all ages, nearly all being from the immediate neighbourhood. They suffered from the general violence of the region and, in many cases, from personal domestic violence at home (84–5). They were all struggling to make ends meet and had daily responsibility for children, grand-children or both. The lives of these women were hard, and it was with this background that they interacted with the church and its spaces (88).

One older lady was still responsible for the day-to-day care of her family, including her grandchildren (44–5, 65–6). She regularly attended Mass where she would sit near the back and follow the service on her own. She felt that many changes in the church in recent years, particularly changes in worship and the more informal approach of the clergy, were taking away the holiness that she remembered and treasured. Once or twice a month she came, on her own or with a friend, to clean the church, especially the sanctuary, the place of the altar and the tabernacle containing the Blessed Sacrament. She would clean the candlesticks and brass ornaments, wash the tiled floor, and polish the wooden altar rails and surrounding furniture. She particularly remembered a time when she and her friend sat on the altar steps during a great storm and, as the wind rushed around the church, she felt especially close to God (179).

The priest at this time was trying to 'move the church forward', as he saw it, including rearrangement of the interior to move the sanctuary from the east end to a space against the north wall. This woman and her friends opposed this move vehemently, seeing it as seriously undermining the sacredness of the sanctuary space that they held so dear. She even threatened to leave if the rearrangement took place.

My student asked her why she came to the church, and the answer was for peace and quiet, to get away from her home, to be on her own with God. She felt that she could be alone with God during worship, even with others present. However, it was when cleaning, up there in the sanctuary, close to the Blessed Sacrament, that she felt she could get really close to God. She could talk to God as she cleaned, she could tell God all her troubles and all her suffering, and God would listen to her as she polished the brass and washed the floor. This, she said, was why she came to church, 'to sit through Mass, or to polish the altar steps and hear the voice of God in the wind outside' (179).

Whatever we may think about the wider implications of this story (and I will return to some of them later), we see in this woman's behaviour a very traditional understanding of sacred space. There, within the church, and most specifically within the sanctuary, as close as possible to the source of 'sacredness', the Blessed Sacrament, this woman could get 'close to God'. It was God's presence, in a very literal as well as in a metaphorical sense, that made this space 'sacred' for this woman. It was, however, only at times when the space was empty of other people that it was truly 'sacred' in this traditional sense, and it was only in opposition to the space of the home – a space of chaos, noise, and violence – that this space of quiet and order could be defined as 'sacred' at all. What we see here, therefore, is the traditional definition of 'sacred space', a space set apart through the presence of the Divine (Knott 2005: 95–104). If we move on to other studies, however, we see other definitions.

## The Spaces of a Methodist Chapel

Let me take you now out of the inner city, to north Norfolk and to the work of a male student (Braddy 2002). He studied a village on the edge of the Norfolk Broads which had been dominated for more than a hundred years by the Methodist church, and was known locally as a 'Methodist village'. The congregation, however, had been declining in numbers over the last fifty or more years and the local Methodists were concerned that their church was going to close. The student was interested in many aspects of the life and faith of this community, but my interest here is in the Methodists' understanding of sacred space.

The areas within and around the church comprised three distinct spaces, each of which could be considered more 'sacred' than the last (134–43). At the front of the church was a schoolroom: a public space and a space that the congregation was keen to use in many ways for the benefit of the village as a whole. The congregation therefore used this space for meetings, for gathering before and after worship, and for the struggling Sunday school. It was also a space where the local people could drop in for coffee on a Wednesday morning, and it provided an alternative to the village hall for 'parties, business meetings and clinics' (140). It had a kitchen and toilets and was being considered for parent and toddler groups, pensioner meetings and even a youth group. This space was at the centre of the congregation's perceived mission to the rest of the village (140–41).

Beyond the hall, however, was the church itself, the worship space of the congregation. This was a traditional Methodist building with pews in neat rows, a gallery for the choir, an organ at the back and a pulpit at the front. Above the pulpit on a plain white wall hung a simple wooden cross, the only visual focal point in the whole area (136). This was a space of stark simplicity, beautifully proportioned but lacking in any 'home comforts', clearly intended for worship. The congregation forbade any group using the hall during the week from entering this space, and would not consider any changes to its layout. This was a space of worship, a sacred space contrasting with the profane space of the hall, and there was a clear boundary, a locked door, between them.

This was the church building, but behind the schoolroom was another space, outside the building, that the Methodists may have considered even more sacred than the worship space itself. This was the Methodist cemetery (142–3), which was unusual since English Methodist chapels do not normally have their own graveyards, but it was full and so closed to new burials. It was therefore a neglected space. Certainly members of the principal families of the congregation were buried there, and their graves were well maintained. However, the location of the cemetery behind the schoolroom, away from the road, and out of sight for most ordinary people, meant that this was a space that was even more inaccessible, and even less visited by ordinary villagers, than the space allocated for worship. This was despite the fact that the village war memorial was also sited in the cemetery. However, as Braddy comments, the memorial 'remained a public commemoration in what was perceived as a private place' (143).

So we have three spaces, one behind the other, each more inaccessible than the last, and considered more sacred the further they are from the road. This is a classic case of 'gradated sacred space', which is part of the discussion of 'sacred space' (J. Z. Smith, 1987: 47–73).

But what was it that made these spaces more or less sacred? It was surely not their relative inaccessibility, or their distance from the road. It was because these spaces were designated as 'sacred' that the number and range of people allowed to enter them were restricted. So we still have to ask: what, in the minds of the congregation, made the worship space, and the graveyard behind the chapel, 'sacred'?

'Worship' is one obvious answer for the middle space, the space set aside specifically for worship, but that does not provide the whole picture. One of the stories about this community brings us closer to a more definitive set of answers. Following a service one Sunday morning, Braddy mentioned to the chapel steward that there had only been about twelve people sitting in a space designed for well over a hundred. How could the congregation worship the living God in such a dead environment? This was totally the wrong question to ask! The steward pointed at different pews, and told the student that

the Methodist Church space contained strong memories of family members who had died. A pew was significant because someone special used to sit there. There was a sense of awe for those who belonged to these families. Their forebears hallowed the space for the continuing of worship. Linked with this was an understanding of the sacrifices of these people as they built the Church, giving generously for the construction and upkeep of the Church. Some were very poor farm labourers. Others saw their inheritance being spent on the maintenance of the Church by their parents (Braddy 2002: 135).

The church was not empty in the minds of the congregation, but full – full of all the people who had ever worshipped there in the hundred years or so of its history. And far from being a 'dead' and 'empty' space, as Braddy came to realize, this was a space fully alive with the people, the history and the memories of the community. Even the cross that dominated the space was remembered more for the sacrifice of a grandfather in whose memory it was given, than for the sacrifice of Christ (137). We have to come back to the question: What made this space 'sacred'?

There are various answers to this question, and I will simply lay them out at this point and leave the question hanging. We could identify the sacredness of the space with God or the divine, as we did with the inner-city Anglo-Catholic church. It was the space where God was worshipped and where the people perhaps came closest to God. That is conjecture, and does not really explain why the graveyard was considered to be more sacred than the worship space. We could follow Belden Lane, writing of sacredness in the American landscape, and identify the sacredness of the space with history, the depth of time that this space had been used for worship, and the sense of communal story that it contained (Lane 1988: 20). We could associate the sacredness of the space with people. This is the language the church steward had used to talk about the 'living' nature of the space when Braddy had described it as 'dead'. It was people from the past who inhabited this space, and their relationship with the living that made it 'sacred'. We could identify the sacred space with memory, following the work of Danièle Hervieu-Léger (2000) and others who see memory as central to any understanding of religion.

These last three suggestions link the sacredness of the worship space with the greater sacredness of the cemetery, each being a space saturated with the stories and memories of people, both the living and the dead, and it was in terms of memory that the concept of sacredness was expressed. I do not at this stage wish to choose between these alternatives, but simply to leave them as possibilities and move on to a very different situation in a small mining community just north of Coventry.

## The Space of the Graveyard

The Anglican vicar of a small former mining town in north Warwickshire had been a successful missionary in Nigeria, and came to this town on his return to England in the early 1990s. For ten years he ministered to the congregation and the people of the town, but in all that time not a single person from the wider community came to join the church. He came to me wanting to know why, and so began an ethnographic study of the religious attitudes of the people of the town (Kimber 2001). The answer to his specific question probably lay in the social structure of the town – the Anglican church was associated historically with the mine owners rather than the workers – and the appalling behaviour of one of his recent predecessors, who used to beat his wife and who sat in his garden at the rectory shooting at homing pigeons as they returned from their races (44–9). It was not this aspect of his research, however, which concerns me here.

On spending a considerable time listening to the ordinary people of the town, who had been miners or were from mining families, Kimber was surprised to find that these people had a very high regard for the Anglican Church, although it was the church building and not the congregation that was the focus for their affection. On investigating further he discovered that it was primarily the graveyard that was important to them (110), and for the first time in his ministry he began to take note of what was happening there every day. On most days one or more of the people from the town would come to the graveyard and tidy up a particular grave, leave new flowers and spend some time standing or sitting near the grave itself (115). When Kimber asked what they were doing he was told that they were 'chatting' to their dead relatives, bringing the dead up-to-date with the latest gossip and seeking their advice on difficult personal or family matters. On enquiring further he discovered that the dead were often consulted and chatted to when important issues in the family were raised. It appeared to be a natural reaction, especially among the women. 'People go up and talk through their problems with the deceased, just as they did in life, and just as they did in life, they sometimes ask for help' (118). It was not just the graveyard that provided a space for this type of communication. In any space where the women were alone and able to find a few moments of peace, the dead could be chatted to. The dead could just as easily be consulted over a cigarette and a cup of tea in the kitchen as they were over flowers in the graveyard.

This behaviour fascinated Kimber, and it forms a large part of his thesis. He was interested in how this process could be developed as part of missionary activity within the community. That is not my concern, but what interests me is the behaviour itself, and most specifically the matter-of-fact nature of it. There was no sense of awe or fear or trepidation in the way these people approached the dead. They described the activity as 'chatting', a very informal register of conversation. They treated the dead, according to their own description, in exactly the same way as they would have treated them when they were alive (118), although there was perhaps a greater sense that once dead these people could do more to help than they ever could when they were alive – at least they would stay still and listen without ever answering back.

But nobody expected miracles, the intervention of the dead, or even the voice of the dead speaking directly to them. This was not the issue. When things worked out well against the odds, then the dead were given some credit. When they did not, it was always the living who were blamed. As people chatted and found an answer to their problems, then the dead were credited with having provided that answer. Nobody talked in terms of 'ghosts' or 'voices' or any other directly supernatural phenomena, although a number of people commented on seeing 'little hints of their presence' such as depressions in cushions, or the radio coming on with no obvious cause (120). The dead were too close, too immediate, too normal for supernatural language. There was nothing, we might say, that was inherently 'sacred' or 'religious' about this chatting to the dead.

What, then, should we say about the nature of sacred space in this context? The first question we might ask is whether we should still be using the word 'sacred'. To answer that we need a more detailed analysis of the situation itself. If we accept that chatting to the dead is in some senses a 'sacred' activity – the dead are clearly non-empirical in the terms that I have presented in previous chapters – then the two locations in which this occurs must be seen as 'sacred spaces'. The real question is whether we are to interpret the chats at the graveside as more normal than with those in the kitchen (or other domestic spaces), or those in the kitchen as more normal than those at the grave. This would help us to understand how people themselves understand the 'sacred'.

What I mean by this is that if we assume that the 'normal' site for chatting to the dead is the graveyard, then we do not have to change our notion of sacred space at all. The chats in the kitchen, for example, simply become an extension of the graveyard, a space that is, for the time of the chat at least, equated with the graveyard, a kind of surrogate graveyard for those who do not have the time to reach the place itself. If this is the case then what I have already said about sacred space in relation to the Methodist context in Norfolk still holds. I suggested that the sacredness of those Methodist spaces could be associated with people, history and memory, all of which function equally well for the graveyard of this town, and by extension for the kitchen. If, on the other hand, we turn this around and assume that the graveyard is simply an alternative site for chats that could happen just as easily in the kitchen, or some other domestic space, then our thinking has to go back to the beginning of our discussion (Knott 2005: 97–9).

## The 'Sacred'

If we turn to Emile Durkheim we find the classic definition of the 'sacred' as 'that which is set apart' (1995: 34–5). This expresses clearly what makes each space sacred in the three contexts that I have just been describing. We could ask what these spaces are set aside for. The obvious example in all three cases might be 'meeting with God, or the dead', or in more abstract terms, 'meeting with the non-empirical other'. This is fine, but it does not tell us anything about the nature of the space itself, and largely provides us with a circular argument: the space is 'sacred' because we meet 'sacred' others there, and these others are considered 'sacred' because we meet them in 'sacred' spaces.

It is more interesting to ask what these spaces are set aside *from*. In the account of the woman at the Anglo-Catholic church, a major feature was the marked contrast between the everyday, chaotic and violent life of the women outside of the church, and the peace, order and tranquillity of their time within it (Schofield 1999: 81–9). The sacred space is defined here in opposition to normal, daily life, what Durkheim might describe as the 'profane'. We can see something similar in the case of the north Warwickshire mining town. I asked whether we should see the graveyard in this case as an alternative to, or an extension of, the kitchen, rather than the other way around. When Kimber listened carefully to the women talking about this kind of behaviour, it was the peace and quiet that was stressed more than the physical nature of the space (2001: 119).

In other words the normal context for chatting to the dead was snatched moments of rest in an otherwise busy and chaotic world, the fag and the cuppa in the kitchen, and the trip to the graveyard was merely an extension of this, a place of greater quiet and order, a place where you would go to deal with really serious problems and for deeper conversations. Again, as with the woman in Birmingham, we have a clear opposition between the chaos and busyness of ordinary lives and the peace and order of these snatched 'sacred' moments. We could also see the dead of the Warwickshire village and the God of the Anglo-Catholic church as structural equivalents. In many ways, what matters is the quiet, the order, the peace and the chance to be alone. Who is spoken to in those spaces, who provides the confidential, intimate 'partner' in the conversation, is largely irrelevant so long as they are not empirically present to disrupt the sense of peace and quiet.

If we look more closely at this relationship with the 'other' in each of these situations, we can perhaps draw some further conclusions. It is clear that both the women in the church and the women in their kitchens are actually engaged in the same kind of activity. They are both taking the opportunity to stand back from difficult lives, to find peace, and to share their problems with a non-respondent other. It is important in both situations that the 'other' is understood to be completely real: this is not an 'imaginary friend' that is being engaged with. While the women in the mining community may, at other times and in other contexts, dismiss completely the idea that the dead are present in this world and can interact with the living, this is a 'situational belief' that is essential for the situation under consideration.

The other element that is essential however, as well as the reality of the 'other', is their non-intervention. As I have already said, the assumption is that the conversation partner does not, and perhaps cannot, answer back. This is particularly important in a context where normal, everyday conversation with human others is so disappointing. Where this everyday conversation is seen as confrontational, consisting largely of shouting, swearing and other verbal violence, and rarely consists of two people listening to each other, then finding a context where some kind of other is known to listen, and to care, is essential. If the only other who can fit that bill is non-empirical, then that is the other that is chatted to.

This leads me on to a third point, that the non-empirical other is considered to be an intimate of the speaker. I am not saying that the other is equal to the respondent – that is not the case: both the dead and God are in some sense 'better' and more powerful than the speaker – but the intimate relationship with that other is essential. This may also explain why the other is different in each case. For the women in the church, God is an intimate, somebody they can converse with on a familiar level, a friend and a listener. For the women in the mining town, God could not be seen in that way. God for them is too powerful, too distant, not interested in the details of their own lives. The dead, however, are clearly intimate, and interested, and they are the others whom these women choose to turn to.

Could we, therefore, say that something similar is going on with the Methodists in Norfolk? Up to a point, I think that we can. The same kind of language is being used of the sacred space itself. The worship space and the graveyard beyond the chapel are both spaces set apart. They are both spaces of quiet and order – with the discourse about the chapel emphasizing 'order', while that relating to the graveyard emphasizes 'quiet'. There is a clear and deliberate attempt to keep these spaces apart, to maintain the quiet and the order, by excluding others and by special techniques of cleaning and maintenance. These are also spaces where the people meet with the non-empirical other, both with God and, once again in this case, with the dead. Of course the register of the communication with these others would not be described by the Methodists themselves as 'chatting', but the familiarity and intimacy expressed in the steward's description of the 'living' chapel certainly mirrors the relationships between the women of the other two contexts and their own chosen 'others'. There is an intimacy and familiarity here, although the study itself did not develop this aspect of the worship. We have no direct evidence from the Methodists, but a great deal of evidence from my previous work on attitudes to worship, and from other students within the wider project, suggests that many people use the worshipping environment as a space for intimate and wide-ranging conversations with God, or Jesus, or the saints, or the dead, of the kind that we have seen with the women in the other examples (Stringer 1999a: 112–120). This is one of the reasons given for why many people go to church, and one of the primary benefits they claim to get out of it.

## Space and Place

This leads me to my final point. Jonathan Z. Smith argues that we need to distinguish between 'space' and 'place' in any discussion of the definition or use of 'sacred space' (1987). 'Space', for Smith, suggests something permanent, somewhere that has been set aside for ritual or other purposes and which takes on a symbolic association of its own. 'Place', on the other hand, is something that is created for a purpose and is unique to that purpose and those who are involved in it. Spaces, such as temples and churches, can be turned into places by use and by the people who frequent them. This is what we have seen with the Methodists, who fill their space with the living dead and so transform it into a place for them to worship. The woman in Birmingham also transforms the space of the sanctuary into a place of communication with God. What is important here is that while the woman draws on generally accepted symbolic markers of the sacred, the presence of the Blessed Sacrament for example, it is not in devotion to the sacrament itself that this space becomes a place for her, but through cleaning and chatting to God. Her place, therefore, is different from that of all the other women of that church, even if it is created within the same space. For the women of the mining community we can see the creation of place even more clearly, whether that is in the kitchen or in the graveyard. It is the activity, the sense of peace and quiet, the chatting to the dead and the creation of a momentary place of order within a wider space of chaos that makes this a 'sacred' place for these women.

What we see in each of these situations is a similar process to that which I have already explored for 'situational belief'. It takes more than just holding beliefs to make those beliefs important: it is the situation within which the belief is held that is essential. And, as I explained in the previous chapter, the fact that the same person can hold contradictory beliefs in different situations, each relevant and true in the situation for which it is held, is what really matters. So it is arguable that the sacredness of space is also situational, dependent on the creation of place by the individuals concerned (Chidester and Linenthal 1995: 6). In the same way we can also talk about the commitment that has to be given to this creation of place for it to be considered 'sacred' by the individual concerned. As with belief statements there is something distinctive about the act of recognizing the non-empirical. If this is true in the case where the non-empirical is simply conceived of, it must be more so when that same non-empirical is engaged with in conversation (Harvey 2005). The sacred place is created where the individual is alone, apart from the non-empirical other, and such places are seldom talked about in everyday conversation. Situational sacred places therefore, like situational beliefs, are part of the religious landscape of many people in England today – albeit a landscape that is hidden from the majority of observers.

## Conclusion

The phenomena I have presented in this chapter should not be considered unusual or rare. I mentioned in Chapter Two that one great joy of ethnographic study is that students come away surprised by what they have found. All three of the incidents mentioned in this chapter include elements that surprised the researcher involved. The most surprising feature identified by the Worship in Birmingham Project was people's admission that they chatted to the dead. Over and over again, from a wide range of circumstances, whether the people studied were members of Christian congregations or outside official religious discourses, some kind of interaction with the dead was discovered. This phenomenon must therefore be widespread within English society, and I will return to it in the next two chapters.

This chapter, however, is not essentially about talking to the dead. The example provided by the work in Birmingham shows that it is not only the dead that are 'chatted' to. For many Christians their relationship with God, or Jesus, or the saints takes a similar form to the intimate chatting to the dead described by others. The language of Jesus as friend, or Mary as an intimate companion and guide, has a similar structure (Stringer 2005: 20–1). What links all these situations, however, is the level of intimacy between the speaker and the non-empirical other that is constructed as the listener. As I said above, this is not some awesome tremendous 'Other' in front of whom the speaker cowers in fear and trembling. The conversation partner in all these contexts is seen as a 'friend', a 'companion', a 'relative', a 'confidant'.

What is also interesting in this context is that many people who claim to have seen the dead or angels or ghosts, in contemporary society, also talk about 'peace' and 'comfort' rather than 'fear' and 'trembling' (Heathcote-James 2001, 2003). To be visited by a dead loved one, or an angel in the form of a dead loved one, a short while after their death is described as a sign of comfort, and confirmation that the loved one has found peace. This is a very different discourse from the traditional ghost story, and different from the concept of other cultures, both contemporary and historical, where ghosts are seen as 'lost souls', forced to wander forever without finding peace.

I will return to this discussion in the following chapter, where the role of Spiritualist churches in inner urban Manchester is considered. All I wish to demonstrate now is that, for most ordinary people who have been engaged in our research projects, the interaction with the non-empirical other is not one of transcendence or awe, but of quiet comforting intimacy. Whether this demonstrates a change in English society, or something much more fundamental about ordinary religious behaviour, I shall leave for my conclusion.

Chapter Five

# Of Star Signs and Soap Operas

As I said in Chapter Two, having completed my PhD at the University of Manchester I worked for five years as a church-related community worker in an inner-urban area of Manchester, just east of the city centre. My official task was to help 13 Anglican churches in this area to develop their work with young families. My actual work consisted of congregational development and helping out with various parent and toddler groups in the neighbourhood.

When I began I was presented with the model of liberation theologians working in the slums of a South American city, as a possible blueprint for my work. These theologians had, I was told, called together groups of young mothers from the slums and read the Gospel to them. They had asked the women to talk about their own lives, and they had brought the Gospel narrative into contact with the personal narratives of the women. The story of the birth of Jesus, for example – a story of a single mother, living in poverty with no home of her own, giving birth in the back of a stable – was said to have spoken directly to the women of the slums, and their response, I was assured, was to rise up and become involved, to set up a support group for single mothers in their neighbourhood and to campaign for more suitable maternity facilities at the local hospital. Wouldn't it be possible, I was asked, to start this same process with the young women of this English inner city?

I tried. I called a group of willing mothers together, and we began to explore their own experiences and to read the biblical stories together. The telling of personal stories was great, they all enjoyed this and we all benefited greatly from it, but the attempt to relate this to the biblical narrative, especially the Christmas story, simply failed to ignite any sparks. Perhaps it was the way I did it, perhaps it was because I was a man, and a woman would have been able to handle the dynamics better, I do not know. One thing that struck me, however, was that this sacred narrative simply did not register. They all knew the Christmas story of course, their kids had performed in nativity plays and they had seen the Christmas cards. It was cute and it was kitsch but it had nothing to say to them personally, except to remind them of roast turkey and the chaos of Christmas Day. There was nothing in the story that had the power to transform these women in the way that it had transformed the women of the South American slum.

In this chapter I want to focus on three situations where ordinary people, specifically women, *do* call on narratives of the non-empirical to help them in their everyday lives. I want to ask how these narratives work, how the women are drawn into engaging with them and the kind of questions or concerns the women expect the narratives to address. The fact that most of the informants involved are women is an important finding, and one that I will come back to in the following chapter. The other point to make, at the beginning of the discussion, is that very few of the women from these case studies are regular church members, in fact most clearly felt alienated from the mainstream churches, and this is also significant.

I will begin therefore with astrology and spiritualism, as this helps us to put the other two cases into context. I will then look at various studies of women in black-majority churches or in other black religious environments, and at women who watch soap operas, relating both of these contexts to Robert Wuthnow's study of people who meet regularly in small groups in the United States (1994). In none of these situations does the narrative have the effect that the story of Jesus' birth was supposed to have on the women of South America, but each shows how ordinary people, and women in particular, draw on such narratives to provide an explanation of, and support for, their everyday lives.

## Seeking Stars

Astrology may seem to be an odd place to begin a discussion of religious narratives. I want to introduce it at this stage, however, because I have had a very clear experience of how astrology works within a small group of women at a parent and toddler group in Manchester. As part of my work for the churches I spent a considerable time at local parent and toddler groups getting to know, chatting with and listening to the local mothers (fathers seldom came!). At first I was, naturally, treated with considerable suspicion. Over time, however, I became an accepted fixture within a couple of groups, although never really part of the intimate discussions between the mothers themselves, always on the edge, an ignored observer rather than a true participant.

It was in this context that I began to pick up conversations about astrology. Looking up 'the stars' in magazines was a regular part of the initial conversation at many meetings. Like the weather and items of local gossip, comparing the stars was a way into conversation, part of the opening gambit. It was also treated with a great deal of scepticism and laughter by the young mothers involved. It was not taken seriously, not something that any of the women appeared to live their lives by, or at least so it appeared on the surface.

As I listened to the women's conversation over time, however, a number of situations emerged when the sceptical, fun and joking approach to magazine astrology began to take a more serious turn. In each case it appeared that one of the women was struck by something in the text of the magazine prediction that spoke to her life, or a woman felt particularly worried by some event or concern that she hoped the stars would address. The tone of the conversation would change slowly and almost imperceptibly, and the words of the magazine were interrogated with much more seriousness.

It was invariably at this point that one of the older women would lean forward and, in something approaching a whisper, suggest that the mother concerned should think of taking a more professional reading. By this stage the tone of the conversation had shifted completely. Joking had ceased, scepticism had gone and something very significant was clearly being discussed. If the mother concerned had a real problem then the older women invariably knew somebody, either locally or in Blackpool or wherever, who could be called upon to provide a clear and definitive reading that would answer the concerned woman's problem. This led on to serious conversations, and negotiations, about the respective merits of known astrologers, and to arrangements for the mother with the problem to make an appointment. Invariably in these conversations the powers of the astrologers were illustrated through the personal experiences of other women present, experiences of where the consultation had proved correct, of where the process had worked. Never were the powers of astrology challenged.

What struck me in these situations, and I witnessed about ten conversations in different groups in this area of Manchester, was the way in which a discourse of scepticism and joking, a discourse that essentially dismissed astrology as no more than a bit of fun, was transformed rapidly into a discourse about astrologers that was serious and firmly believed by all those concerned, with the level of commitment that I have already suggested is essential for all situational belief. Much in this situation reminded me of the discussions of witchcraft in France as recounted by Jeanne Favret-Saada (1980). Favret-Saada, through a detailed analysis of her fieldwork, demonstrates the need for an 'annunciator' in cases of witchcraft accusations, a person who can link a series of misfortunes together and present them as a coherent narrative of witchcraft to the family under attack (8). Before the annunciator has spoken, nobody claims to take the idea of witchcraft seriously, and the most common public register for the discourse on witchcraft is that of joking scepticism. It is only when the annunciator proclaims that the individual, or more usually a family, is the victim of witchcraft that the tone changes and a new perspective on both the situation and belief in witchcraft emerges. It is the power of speaking, the announcing of the 'deadly words', that makes witchcraft a reality in Favret-Saada's analysis (9–12).

The same is clearly true in the cases of astrology that I witnessed. The older women act as 'annunciators' encouraging the younger women with problems to recognize the underlying narrative of their misfortune and to consult professional astrologers whom they may not have known previously. Suddenly astrology can seem a very serious and perfectly sensible response to a whole range of situations and issues faced by the mothers involved.

There is an element of 'situational belief' acting in this situation, as I have already suggested, but this example also illustrates how women who may normally have little serious interest in the paranormal, the traditionally religious, or the non-empirical, can very quickly be encouraged to take all of these very seriously indeed in particular circumstances. The encouragement to visit an astrologer, however, is just one of a number of possible outcomes of this kind of discussion. As well as astrologers, I have heard women in similar situations being encouraged to attend a local Spiritualist church and, on one occasion, a local black Pentecostal church, for the same reasons that they might be encouraged to visit an astrologer. I have no idea what the outcome of the visit to the Pentecostal church was, but I did listen in on a couple of conversations that followed visits to the Spiritualists.

None of the women involved were regular members of the Spiritualist community. Even the annunciators had only had a fleeting acquaintance with the church, or knew somebody else who had. These are not women, therefore, who are part of regular Spiritualist congregations. Spiritualism, it was proposed, would give a woman the opportunity to make contact with somebody who was already dead who, it was thought, could help with their current problems. The assumptions behind the proposal, and the structure of the conversation, were exactly the same as for the visit to an astrologer. What was being offered was a pragmatic solution to a very specific problem, not an invitation into a new way of life.

Only one of the visits to the Spiritualist church appeared to be successful. The unsuccessful visit, however, was not discussed at length. A simple statement of the visit, and the failure of anything to happen, led to a rapid change in the subject of conversation. Nobody seemed to be particularly struck by the success or failure of the visit for others in the room, nor overwhelmed by the situation in itself. If it did not work for the woman concerned, it was dismissed and other tactics were explored. It was only when there was a 'successful' outcome, therefore, that the details of the event and its impact on the women were discussed at length, and even here the emphasis was entirely on the outcome, in terms of the solution to the original problems, rather than on the events that had occurred at the Spiritualist church itself.

What this highlights to me is the very pragmatic attitude of the women involved. They were looking for something that would 'work' in the sense that it would sort out an immediate problem. They were not looking for a religious experience or searching for a new moral code. The problems they took to the astrologers or the Spiritualist church were mundane and practical. There were questions about the illness of a child, or concerns about a situation at work, or fears about a violent boyfriend. These concerns were part of everyday life but a part that had, for that particular moment, taken on a size and significance that was out of proportion. These were problems that had come to dominate the lives of the women, problems that ordinary practitioners – doctors, health visitors, social workers – could not offer solutions to. There was nothing particularly 'spiritual' about these problems. They were, however, beyond the control of the women involved, and they had happened by chance. The issues were of absolute importance to the women at the time they were raised, and the women needed to have immediate answers. They were therefore happy to explore a range of possibilities, and even to suspend their disbelief, in order to find the solutions they needed.

It is in this context, therefore, that the visits to astrologers or the Spiritualists have to be seen. There was no sense in which these women 'believed' in the power of the stars or the dead to influence their lives in any general sense. They were generally highly agnostic on what happens to people after death, changing their views in response to circumstances in the way that I have explained in Chapter Three. It was not through any confidence in the efficacy of the Spiritualists or astrologers themselves, or in any wider body of beliefs, that these women sought answers to their specific problems. It was the suggestion from one set of, generally older, women that this was one context in which answers had been forthcoming in the past that led other women to try it out.

What is also clear, however, is that these women were not particularly surprised or frightened by the possibility that dead relatives, usually mothers or grandmothers or much-loved aunts – other women who were close to them already – would speak to them through a medium. This possibility was accepted, and the reality of the communication went unquestioned. In stories of the events little was said about the actual words used by the medium or, for that matter, the exact content of the message from the dead. It was the reality of contact, and the sense that somebody who had been close to them was still watching over them, that appeared to matter. In this sense these women were exactly like those in the various examples that I offered in the previous chapter. Once an intimate contact with a non-empirical other was made, the importance of the problem appeared to recede and the women began to feel confident again about their future.

It is interesting that the topics determining the conversations with the dead in north Warwickshire were exactly the same as those which led the women in Manchester to consult astrologers or spiritualists. It was primarily family matters, issues and problems that had arisen in everyday life; illness, particularly of children, worries about work, or the lack of it, financial problems and aspects of relationships between men and women. It was the range of standard everyday issues that face everybody in their day-to-day lives. These were ordinary problems, nothing special or spectacular.

What is interesting about the mining village community, however, when compared with my evidence from Manchester, was that chatting to the dead appeared to be much more common and ordinary. It was a regular part of life, the thing you did when you had problems. The dead who were consulted were the same kind of close family members mentioned by the Manchester women, but whereas the latter needed the intervention of an annunciator and the context of a Spiritualist meeting to reach out to the dead, the people of the mining town lived alongside the dead continuously and turned to them whenever there was a problem or issue they wanted to talk through (Kimber 2001: 117–19).

In the previous chapter I highlighted the very ordinary nature of this communication: it was not seen to involve anything remotely transcendental or extraordinary. The dead, for these informants, are a very imminent part of everyday life. This is not so clearly the case for the women in Manchester, although from the way the women talked about contacting the dead they did not seem to regard the experience as significantly 'transcendental'. The dead themselves were seen as mundane and ordinary, just as they had been in life. But they were not so much a part of everyday life as in the mining village, and more effort was needed to contact them.

Other contexts for conversations with the dead tend to fall somewhere between these two poles. The reasons for talking to the dead and the issues brought by people for consultation with the dead were always much the same: basic, pragmatic problems thrown up by everyday life that could not be easily solved; uncertainties and worries faced by the people concerned. The kind of relationship people had with the dead they consulted were also very similar: usually the dead were known to them and were of the previous generation, or older members of the person's own generation. More women were consulted than men, and it was primarily women who did the consulting.

The times and places where the dead were consulted, however, did vary, and there was a continuum between the exclusivity of the Spiritualists, as with the Manchester women, and the everyday contact of the kitchen, as with many in the Warwickshire mining town. The graveyard was by far the most common place to come and chat to the dead, and this often meant making a special journey and setting aside a particular time in a busy schedule. This also determined how important the issues discussed were to the people concerned. It took effort to make the journey and a decision to set aside the time, so the issues had to be of considerable concern to those who chatted to the dead. This is important, and I will come back to it below. At this point, however, I want to provide other examples.

## Soap Operas and Womanist Theologies

In the late 1990s I was asked to examine a thesis on the role of soap operas in pastoral care. The student, Lucy D'Aeth, had used ethnography to study the way in which a group of lesbian viewers used storylines in soap operas to deal with their own lives and construct their own identities (D'Aeth 1999). Her study points out that the narrative structure of soap operas provides a perfect context for dealing with real life. In most plays, films, novels or other forms of fiction the narrative structure, however complex, will always contain a beginning, a middle and an end. This is not the case for soap operas (Mumford 1995: 67–93). As soon as one storyline reaches some kind of resolution, another begins, and yet another sees an incremental development on its own way towards resolution. There is no beginning or ending, just as in life. Among our friends and family, different narrative threads are developing at different rates. Some people are undergoing crisis, some are making new starts, and some are experiencing the ending of part of their lives. The soap opera, therefore, mirrors reality in a way that few other fictional forms do and therefore, according to D'Aeth, can be used as a framework for pastoral care.

One of the points her thesis makes which is particularly relevant to the present discussion, is that the ongoing, even relentless nature of soap operas means that substantial, lasting or final forms of transformation rarely occur. People in the stories change, of course, and even grow, emotionally and personally, through the series of events that occur to them; but having survived a particular crisis and faced a particularly difficult period in their life, there is no sense that a character can, in the language of other fiction, 'live happily ever after' knowing that this experience has changed them fundamentally and permanently for the better. After the inevitable rest, to give the actors a break, the character will inevitably face another crisis some episodes later and, once again, find all their personal resources tested in a new (and, to the viewer, equally gripping) situation.

Things do change or develop in soap operas, but things never stop. Once one crisis is averted, the next is simply waiting around the corner. 'Soap opera', according to D'Aeth, 'reflects a community where struggles are not ultimately resolved, but where life continues and resistance, rather than ultimate victory, is the goal' (1999: 139). That is very much the way many people, including the mothers I was listening to in Manchester, understand their lives.

One of the sources D'Aeth draws upon to make a link between soap opera and theology is the work of 'Womanist' theologians (231–35), in order to trace a link between the narrative style of soap operas and the narrative structure of many African-American women's lives. 'Womanist theology' is a form of theology that has been developed among black women, initially in the States and increasingly in Britain, the West Indies, South America and elsewhere. Womanist theology recognizes the double oppression that black women face, because of their gender and their colour, and rejects not only traditional white male theologians but also older feminist theologians (because of their perceived racial bias as white women) and the writing of black male theologians (who are seen as seldom attuned to the needs of black women).

Delores Williams is one of the leading exponents of Womanist theology, and her book *Sisters in the Wilderness* (1993) is one of the most significant texts of the movement. In it Williams identifies the liberationist underpinning of most feminist and Black theology, and claims that this does not easily reflect the everyday experience of black women. The experiences of black women, she argues, follows a narrative structure that does not lead to easy resolution, but moves them from crisis to crisis without their ever stopping to take stock or reflect. To this extent the narrative structure that Williams identifies is exactly the same as that demonstrated by D'Aeth in her studies of soap opera. Womanist theology, Williams claims, has to address this narrative of continuing crisis rather than offering the unrealistic hope of resolution and transformation. This is not to say that Womanist theology should not have a liberationist element: it should, and it does. But the liberation must be found within the narrative of ongoing crises rather than within the narrative of transformation and a 'happy ever after' conclusion.

A number of my recent students have been undertaking ethnographic work with black-majority congregations (Schofield 1999), with black members of white-majority congregations (Smith 2005) or with other forms of black spirituality (Lewis 2007). While all these works have emphasized the importance of Womanist theologies in providing a context for the ethnographic work, each has begun with a process of listening to what the black women involved in the study actually have to say and then extrapolating from this to engage with the wider theological context.

In one such study, Jennifer Smith worshipped with, and tried to understand, a black-majority Methodist congregation in north Birmingham (Smith 2005). She was particularly interested in the meaning of 'holiness' within the congregation, and used a number of techniques – telling, showing and doing – in order to understand how members of the congregation themselves understood 'holiness'. It is in relation to telling, and particularly with reference to language and the role of God in the women's lives, that the narrative structure of their engagement with the non-empirical can be seen.

Smith (2005) begins with a verse-story that one of the women told about her mother's death, where a dying woman, the speaker's mother, named herself for Jesus as he came to meet her at her death:

> She called me by her bedside, and she said ...
> 'I am going home to Jesus,'
> and 'Take care me Jesus now.'

But the most important and the most shocking thing to me ...
'Lord Jesus, my name is Viola Rice!
I am coming home Lord Jesus.' (Smith 2005: 43)

Smith uses this text to describe how the women in the church talked of, and to, Jesus. The naming 'Viola Rice', is related to Jacquelyn Grant's idea of a 'theology of somebodiness' (Grant 1989: ix). There is a degree of intimacy and friendliness in the relationship that is two-sided, a view we have already explored in the previous chapter. More importantly here is the idea of Jesus as a co-sufferer with the women. As one woman said, 'I think I see the goodness of God because I live on my own ... God keeps me! He keeps me! Because I ain't got not strength no power on my own, it the power of God that moves in you, that keeps you going, innit.' (Smith 2005: 46).

Finally there is the idea of God as a trickster, that God bides his time but always gets back at the rich and powerful in some way, and usually at the most unexpected moment. Smith sums up her argument by claiming that 'God as they know and re-know him is an intimate comfort and friend, a home in present exile, a co-suffering saviour, and a trickful help for the less powerful.' (50)

In another study Marjorie Lewis (2007) undertook an ethnographic study of women involved in the Assur Asset Society, an Africanist religion based on the mythologies of Ancient Egypt. The society is only open to people of African origin and has a sophisticated and elaborate series of beliefs and rituals. The boundaries of the society are carefully controlled, but Lewis was privileged to gain access not only to members of the society but also to the rituals and retreats run by it. In her discussion of the 'spirituality' expressed within the society she stresses the mundane and everyday nature of the issues addressed. There is a salvific element to the religion, including the possibility of a person developing through a series of spiritual states and becoming divine. However, for many of the ordinary women involved this is not the aspect of the religion that most appeals to them, but rather the ability to meet in an environment that recognizes their cultural identity and allows them to express their own concerns and troubles. The society also, through its rituals and retreats, provides support and advice to these women in order to help them cope with the troubles of their lives. Lewis goes on to discuss a number of interviews with black Christian women. Her conclusion is that regardless of the religious framework, black women are drawn to a 'black women's spirituality' in which support for the everyday crises of life is central. Once again, therefore, we see an emphasis on the ongoing, open-ended narrative of the soap opera rather than the transformative 'happy-ever-after' narrative usually associated with mainstream Christianity.

## The Domestication of God

Up to this point the evidence that I have adduced relates primarily to women, and particularly to women who would be considered marginal in one way or another: young single mothers from inner-city areas and members of black Christian congregations or black religious groups. How widely is this kind of crisis-to-crisis narrative structure seen in other contexts? One interesting example comes from a very different context. This is Robert Wuthnow's (1994) work on small groups in the United States.

Wuthnow set out to study the development of such small groups. He wanted to test theories of the decline of community and see whether small groups created an alternative to the older models of family or neighbourhood; he also wanted to chart the impact of small groups on American spirituality (9–11). Wuthnow did not set out specifically to study Christian small groups or small groups associated with churches, and his book also refers to other kinds of groups: Alcoholics Anonymous and other 'twelve-step' groups, political pressure groups and even reading circles (64–76). It seems, however, that the vast majority of small groups meeting in the States are church-related, and most people who join them are conservative Christians. This makes his comments on the development of spirituality in the groups more interesting to us.

Evangelical Christianity has been traditionally understood as transformative in its narrative structure, emphasizing conversion and the need for change in the individual, as well as stressing the importance of prayer and the positive outcomes from true prayer in the lives of those who practise it. This kind of narrative existed in the groups Wuthnow studied, but it was not the most significant narrative he saw at work. Small groups, he discovered, tend to encourage their members to look in on themselves (36–40). This does not mean that the people do not engage with their churches or get involved in outreach and social service work. But the conversations within the group were focused primarily on the individuals in the group itself, their daily lives and the many little problems that beset them (173–82). The groups are seen to support individuals in the daily trials of life, to give them a chance to share with like-minded people the issues in work or family life that really concern them. God, Wuthnow suggests, no longer becomes the one who interferes in big ways, demanding great changes and total transformation. God is approached in order to find a parking space, to care for a sick child, to help with a petty squabble at work and so on (239–42). God and the sacred have, in Wuthnow's terms, become 'domesticated' (255).

What we see here, therefore, is a development of a soap opera type of narrative structure within the small group (289–310). The fact that members meet regularly and see each other through from one crisis to the next, and, within the cast of characters that make up the group, deal with a series of overlapping and never entirely ending storylines, means that the group acts in many ways like a soap opera made real. It is not surprising, therefore, that the spirituality developed to engage with this focuses on the minor crises of life and the everyday troubles of the people concerned, a spirituality that is both supportive and pragmatic.

The social make-up of the groups Wuthnow studied is very diverse. He stresses that there is no one social class, no one racial group and no one region of the country that is more widely represented than any other (46–9). Small groups have reached all parts of America. However, we do have to ask whether they, and the spirituality that they encourage, are a uniquely American phenomena. One British study that considers this in some detail is by Abby Day, a PhD student at Lancaster University (Day 2006). Day observed women's prayer groups in Yorkshire, and was struck by the similarities between her own findings and those expressed by Wuthnow. She found the Yorkshire groups to be also inward-looking, and also involved in the 'domestication' of God.

The parent and toddler groups discussed earlier are also 'small groups' in Wuthnow's definition, since they meet regularly to provide support and care for the women involved. It should not surprise us, therefore, if the kind of spirituality that they exhibit is of the type found in Wuthnow's groups; but for these women astrology and Spiritualism provide a more recognizable context for this spirituality than that of traditional Christianity. D'Aeth was also involved in the ethnographic study of a small group, a lesbian support group in London. The members of the black congregations discussed by Smith and Lewis also form themselves into small groups as the basis of their engagement with the divine. The structure of the narratives, therefore, the content of the issues related to the spiritual, and the kind of solutions that are sought, are common to the many small groups we have considered in this chapter.

## Coping and Transformative Religions

When I reflected on the experience of the small group of women I had gathered together in order to recreate, in inner-urban Manchester, what had been achieved in the slums of South America, I recalled the work of Michael Taussig (1987). Taussig is an American anthropologist who undertook fieldwork in Colombia. His main interest was in the ritual context of terror, and the way 'montage' in drug-induced healing rituals enabled ordinary people to deal with the very real terrors of the Colombian death squads. It was not this aspect of his work, however, that I recalled. It was a point he made, almost in passing, that most of the images of Our Lady which hold a special place in South American religion had been 'discovered' by Native Americans (188–209). These images, he argued, therefore contained something of the power, the ambiguity and the danger of the Native American people themselves, especially for the black and white communities that venerated the images.

Taussig demonstrates a symbolic and cultural world in which images of, and relationships with, Mary hold real power for people. This is true also for those who have rejected Catholicism for some form of Pentecostalism (Martin 1990). It is part of the cultural matrix of the societies involved, deeply rooted in their history and common narrative. When the women of the South American slum, therefore, are told that their story reflects and interacts with that of Mary, as described in the biblical narrative, then something of the power and significance of Mary as an icon is transferred to the women themselves, and they are transformed by the sheer power of the juxtaposition. In the case of the women in Manchester, however, Mary does not hold any such associations or relevance. Their primary image is that of the cute Christmas card nativity scene, an image of Mary that has been systematically sucked dry of any symbolic or spiritual power it might ever have had. There is nothing to resonate with their own lives, no power on which to draw in order to transform their own existence.

It was against this background that I began to develop the distinction between 'transformative' and 'coping' religions. The image of Mary in the context of South America formed part of the narrative of a transformative religion; it had the power to change the lives of the women concerned and to provide new energy and new insights (Nagle 1997: 99–115). The women in Manchester had no such notion of 'transformative religion'. A local Anglican priest described their attitude to change and development as 'militant apathy'; they were insistent that no amount of government money or charitable schemes would ever make any difference to their community or their lives (Stringer 2004: 59–60). This did not mean, however, that they had no notion of 'religion'.

All the other examples I have presented in this chapter point to another kind of narrative, another form of religion. This is what I have defined as 'coping religion', a religious discourse that enables ordinary people to cope with the stresses and strains of life as they live it. In the case of the women from the mother and toddler group it enables them to survive from day to day, to deal with concerns about where the next meal is coming from or how to cope with a sick child, a violent partner, or an oppressive landlord. In the case of the Womanist tradition as expressed by Williams, it enables women to cope with the realities of racism and sexism, and with the violence that so often accompanies each form of oppression. In the case of Wuthnow's small groups, the pressures of everyday life may not be so dramatic – the problem of where to park the car, or a minor irritation at work – but the narratives and the domestic spirituality of the small groups also enables their constituents to cope.

When I presented some of this material to a group of Catholic clergy from the Archdiocese of Liverpool in 2001, I was accused of being defeatist and even Thatcherite, of justifying the status quo. However, the clergy in the audience failed to recognize that in defining these two forms of religion I was not advocating one over the other, but simply trying to demonstrate that both forms exist and that in the real everyday world of their parishes, as with England in general, the coping form of religion is actually far more prevalent than the transformative. That, I suggest, is what the various studies explored in this chapter have demonstrated.

If we link the idea of 'coping religions', therefore, with the ideas of the previous chapters we can see a model of religion that is very different from the one assumed by the social scientists and other academics in the definitions that I presented in Chapter One. In Chapter Three I argued that religion for many people in contemporary English society is seldom coherent and systematic; people draw on the belief statements they need in order to address specific situations as and when they arise. In Chapter Four I suggested that chatting with the non-empirical other, whether in the form of God or the dead, is common in English society and that the non-empirical is consequently seen as mundane, approachable, normal and commonplace.

In this chapter, I have suggested that what is brought into those conversations, the reasons for approaching the non-empirical and drawing on belief statements, are themselves fairly mundane. These processes are not about changing the world, or transforming the individual. Conversations with the non-empirical relate to the everyday questions of ordinary life and provide security, support and hope – a means to get through another day, and a strategy to cope with life. This understanding demands a significant redefinition of religion. However, prior to that I need to consider one aspect of the ethnological methodology used to generate the data underpinning my conclusion: its apparent gender bias.

Chapter Six

# On Gender

One of the features that will immediately strike the reader working through the previous three chapters is that almost all the examples involve women. Is this significant? That is the question I wish to address in this chapter before drawing broader conclusions on the definition of religion in my final chapter.

The question of the place of women in the studies underlying this text, and in the kind of religious practice outlined, is not as straightforward as it may seem. There are various explanations for the predominance of women in religious practice, and it is not easy to decide which is most significant. It may be that the contexts in which the studies were undertaken, largely within or on the edge of Christian congregations, are contexts dominated by women. Our statistical information clearly indicates that women outnumber men in Christian congregations by about two to one (Bruce 1995: 43). It is not surprising therefore that most of those who have been listened to by the researchers are women. If this is true then the predominance of women is of little real significance, and we can simply say that more work needs to be done in order to find the men in these contexts and to check the results against their experiences. I am not sure, however, whether this is entirely true. It was not just within the Christian congregations that women predominated in these studies. In inner-city Manchester I was working primarily with young families, which in that context meant young mothers with their children. Most of my time was spent in talking and listening to women. The same is true for Braddy's (2002) work in Norfolk, although in a slightly different context, and with Kimber's (2001) work in North Warwickshire. It was not just within the churches that women predominated; it was also within the communities being studied.

So could we argue, going back to Chapter Two, that it is the methodology of ethnography that brings women's voices to the fore? Certainly many feminist ethnographers would argue that in the past the predominance of male ethnographers meant women were rarely heard (Okley 1996: 211–14). This, however, was largely in the context of studies in other countries. In studies that have applied ethnography to the situation of rural (and some inner-urban) communities in Britain there is no doubt that women's voices have been dominant even when the ethnographer is male (Young and Willmott 1957, Strathern 1981). There are a number of possible reasons for this, but perhaps the most significant is that the women are around the communities when the ethnographers visit. For most of the day the men are involved with work, and if the ethnographers spend time listening to the people who are available, then they will inevitably spend time listening to women. Once again Braddy's and Kimber's experience, as well as my own, confirms this phenomenon in the different communities we studied.

If this is the case, however, is it the end of the story? Is it simply the vagaries of method that have led to an accidental emphasis on women in the studies I have presented, or is there something more fundamental at work? Are the kind of religious practices I have highlighted more common among women, or do they represent a woman's approach to religion? If this were the case then the argument I wish to present in my final chapter concerning the definition of religion would only be relevant for women. Such a claim, therefore, needs to be tested, and that is the purpose of this chapter.

I want first to separate out the wider claim into its constituent parts. It is possible that each of the religious practices that I have considered over the previous three chapters is specific to, or predominant among, women. It is also possible that the underlying religious orientation, the consensual view of the three chapters seen together, is predominantly a women's view of religion. I want to explore each of these possibilities in turn, and then come back to the wider issues in my conclusion. I will begin, therefore, by focusing on the specific issues raised in the previous three chapters: situational belief, attitudes to space and narratives associated with soap operas and astrology. I will then move on to examine what I have described in the last chapter as 'coping religions' in general. In doing this I will move beyond the ethnographic or qualitative methods and draw on evidence that has a more far-reaching quantitative basis.

## Situational Belief

I have been exploring the idea of situational belief in a number of different forms and contexts for over fifteen years. It emerged as part of my doctoral research when I was trying to discover how members of the congregation of an Anglican Church in the centre of Manchester understood their worship (Stringer 1999a: 168–96). I developed the idea of 'belief statements' from Martin Southwold (1983) and related this to the concept of 'ritual statements' in worship (Stringer 1999a: 188–9). Later I developed the idea of situational belief more theoretically for an introductory module on the anthropology of religion at Birmingham University. I needed some way of introducing the concept of 'belief' and realized there was very little in the anthropological literature that would help me to do this. The resulting lecture worked so well that I wrote it up for the *Journal of the Anthropological Society of Oxford* as 'Towards a situational theory of belief' (1996), and it is a version of that paper that appears as Chapter Three of this book.

The reason I am presenting the intellectual history of this chapter is that it is only in the context of this particular text that the question of gender has arisen. In its original context, the inner-urban Anglican Church, I was quite happy to suggest that the male members of the congregation used belief statements just as much as the women. It was certainly the case that the particular group that initially interested me in the possibility of situational belief met after communion on Wednesday lunchtimes, and attracted an older female constituency. The inner controlling team of the church, however, were primarily men, and it was against this group that I tested my ideas at the time (Stringer 1999a: 169). I was aware that the women of the lunchtime communion group were not educated in traditional theological thinking, and may have had a more 'popular' attitude to their faith than the men of the inner core. The controlling team did contain some with a degree in theology, who were achievers in various intellectual fields. I therefore reasoned that if this inner core also used situational beliefs, and such behaviour was not restricted to the older women, then my theory would be more plausible.

It was clear in the original context that independent belief statements, unrelated to each other and sometimes blatantly contradictory, were also related to the construction of worship: once again, blocks of ideas did not always fit smoothly together to form one coherent act of worship, but came together as a kind of montage to create a stimulating and exciting worshipping environment. The thought-processes of the congregation, I argued, related closely to the ritual practice they were engaged in and this, I suggested, was significant (1999a: 188–92). The ritual practice was in the hands of the inner core and so was an essentially male construct. Gender, therefore, did not seem to be an issue in this context, at least not in relation to the question of whether situational belief was gender-specific.

When I came to generalize these ideas beyond the initial fieldwork for the published article, I also failed to identify any gender bias in my thinking. The example I took as the starting point for the *JASO* paper, the church-based study group discussing requiems and reincarnation (Stringer 1996: 217–19), was perhaps even more mixed in gender than the various groups from the Anglican church that had got me thinking in the first place. The study group was made up of long-term members of the congregation in question, with a small number of newer members who had drifted into the church because of other available activities. Both the traditional members and the newcomers were almost equally split between men and women, and both men and women contributed to the discussion of death and reincarnation. There was no suggestion, therefore, that what I was defining as 'situational belief' was something that was specific to women, and this did not occur to me as I developed the various anthropological and sociological ideas that contribute to Chapter Three.

Martin Southwold (1983), Dan Sperber (1974, 1982) and others whose work I draw on for that chapter, fail to indicate whether their ideas are gender-specific. They present their theories as if they refer to all those comprising the society they are studying or, in the case of Sperber in particular, for all people everywhere. Only Geoffrey Ahern stresses the gender of his informants, and in his case these are primarily older men (1987). Gender therefore was not an issue in constructing the notion of 'situational belief'. This does not mean, however, that it is not a gendered concept. Probably the issue of gender was not raised previously because the vast majority of the authors I have drawn on are male and never thought to raise the question of gender bias; this is more likely than the possibility that situational belief represents a truly gender-neutral concept.

If we turn the question around, however, there is likely to be considerable evidence that the more systematic approaches to religion, as exemplified by philosophical speculation and the construction of creeds, are decidedly 'male' approaches, and indeed most of the texts containing these approaches are written by men. Speculation on the differences between male and female brains suggests that men tend to try and fit everything together to form a system, more so than women, although some of this work has been seriously questioned (Lincoln 1996).

Whether or not there is any truth to these theories, I suggest that the proportion of men who become obsessed by the systematic nature of their religion is also relatively small. Clifford Geertz is supposed to have said that 90 per cent of any society is irreligious. What he meant by this was that most members of any society simply go along with whatever dominant discourse is presented for making sense of their lives. Only ten per cent ask the philosophical and theological questions that challenge these assumptions. If it is these ten per cent who produce the systematic structures of religion, and even if all ten per cent are male, then that still leaves 50 per cent of society (the women) who hold some kind of situational belief, along with a further 40 per cent who would all be male. This suggests that situational belief in itself is not a specifically gendered approach, and indeed most of the ethnographic evidence supports this assumption.

## Communing with the Dead, Astrology and Soap Operas

If we move on from situational belief to the other elements I have explored, I shall change the order of the discussion from that of the preceding chapters. The question of gender bias in situational belief relates primarily to the central purpose and understanding of the concept. The question of gender bias in relation to space is much more complex because of the nature of our data. The question of gender bias in relation to conversations with the dead, turning to the stars and watching soap operas can be tested through other, quantitative, data that has been collected over time. It is to this quantitative data that I now wish to turn.

There are various studies showing that the practices described are common in British society. This data has been obtained by various means, including ethnography, and can be regarded as reasonably reliable. So it is possible to test whether each of the practices I have taken as examples of 'religious activity' in the last three chapters are specific to women, or whether they have a wider constituency.

If we begin with the watching of soap operas, we could easily argue from the evidence that the majority of those who watch are women (Hobson 1980, 1982, Mumford 1995). As Dorothy Hobson says:

'Many of the characters in the series *Coronation Street* and *Crossroads* are women who themselves have to confront the "problems" in their "everyday" lives, and the resolution or negotiation of these problems within the drama provides points of recognition and identification for the women viewers.' (1980: 113)

However, the evidence suggests that a significant number of men also watch soap operas. Actually I am not suggesting that watching soap operas is a religious activity in any definition of the term. I introduced the idea simply to highlight the kind of narrative structure present both in soap operas and in various forms of religious discourse. There is no accurate way of measuring the prevalence of any specific type of religious discourse, but a measure of the numbers who watch soap operas could be interesting. The data suggests that the narrative structure underlying soap operas is more widely appreciated by women than by men. Many of those who watch soap operas, however, may also read romantic novels, especially the women (Radway 1984) and such stories typify the narrative structure I have labelled 'transformative', so this data may not be very helpful.

Again, the reading and consulting of horoscopes in a magazine or newspaper does not of itself suggest that the person in question is engaging with the non-empirical. They may not 'believe', they may be having 'a bit of fun', or they may be just acting out of habit. Susan Blackmore and Marianne Seebold (2000) discovered that 70 per cent of the students they questioned read their horoscopes regularly, while a 1996 Gallup poll claims that only 25 per cent believe that the position of the stars and planets affects people's lives. Another poll in 2000 discovered that 17 per cent had tried tarot readings or other forms of fortune-telling, and 16 per cent had tried astrology (presumably asking for a reading as opposed to simply looking up the stars in a newspaper or magazine). However, only 2 per cent of the sample saw each of these as important in living out their lives (Bruce 2002: 81). As I showed in the previous chapter, it is when the casual discussion of the regular horoscope reading in the popular press leads to a suggestion that the individual in question consults a professional astrologer that some kind of transition takes place. It is also clear that of those who do consult an astrologer, the vast majority are women (Blackmore and Seebold 2000).

We could extend this analysis to other activities that have been described as 'new age', 'wellbeing' or 'holistic milieu' practices. They might include astrology or tarot readings and other forms of fore-telling, and they may also include a range of healing practices, meditation, relaxation techniques and other more recognizably religious activities (Heelas and Woodhead 2005: 90–4). It is not clear that every practice that could be classified as 'wellbeing' would come within the remit of what I am calling 'coping religions' – that may be part of a different argument. What is clear, however, is once again the preponderance of women involved in these practices, more so than in the traditional religions. Paul Heelas and Linda Woodhead's study in Kendal found that 80 per cent of those involved in what is described as the 'holistic milieu' are women, while other studies show that women make up only 60 per cent of those involved in the 'congregational domain' (Bruce 1995: 43).

When it comes to communication with the dead, either in everyday life or at the graveside, then statistics are much more difficult to come by. We could ask, for example, what proportion of those who visit graveyards are women. The figures suggest that, once again, the majority are women, but men are well represented (Kimber 2001).

What we do not know from the quantitative studies that have been undertaken is what these people do once they arrive at the graveside. Do they simply rearrange the flowers, or do they 'chat' with their dead loved ones? It might also be possible to include visits to other memorial sites, to where ashes have been scattered or to a memorial bench or some similar place, but once again it is almost impossible to know what occurs at these spaces.

Another possibility is to look at the data on those who have claimed to physically see or hear the dead. One of my students, Emma Heathcote-James, undertook a serious study of such sightings and collected a significant amount of data (Heathcote-James 2003). In her analysis the proportions of men and women are much as we have seen for many of the other practices I have mentioned: there are more women who have seen loved ones, but there are a significant number of men as well. If we assume that men are probably less likely to talk about these things than women, then we may even be able to argue that the proportions are about equal. However, once again, this is not quite the practice I am referring to with the term 'chatting to the dead'. In most of the cases we know from our ethnographic research the dead do not actually appear, nor are they heard to respond by the individuals involved. There is no data, so far as I am aware, of the number of people who 'chat' with the dead, but from the range of seminars and other environments where either I, or my students, have presented some of this material, along with our ethnographic evidence, it seems clear that this practice is very widespread, and undertaken equally by men and women.

Finally in this section, I wish to consider the data collected by Robert Wuthnow on participation in small groups (1994). One of the features that struck him was how many men were involved. The proportions are about equal – 44 per cent of American women join small groups, compared with 36 per cent of men. If we argue that the religious discourse and sensibility expressed in these American groups is similar to the kind of religious expression I define as 'coping religion', then it should be clear that this is not a gendered practice in any obvious way. Whether the evidence that Wuthnow provides can fully justify this claim, however, must remain doubtful. It is clear that the coping narratives of religion are only one aspect of the small groups he discusses, albeit an important aspect, but it is never really clear whether this aspect is focused more on the women or the men, and the material that Wuthnow provides does not allow us to make further enquiries. We have to suggest, therefore, that while the quantitative studies can provide a useful insight they cannot of themselves answer the questions I am posing here.

## Space and the Domestication of Religion

If we now come back to the question of sacred space we see that Chapter Four raised a different kind of question from Chapters Three and Five. In that Chapter I used discourses about space to ask whether religion was always concerned with the transcendent. I suggested that many of the spaces where people conversed with the dead, or met with the non-empirical, were in fact very ordinary, even domestic, hence the joint reference to 'kitchen' and 'graveyard'. However, if we are to describe 'sacred' space with terms such as 'domestic', this inevitably suggests that there may be a gendered element to the discussion of sacred space (Gullestad 1984).

There is considerable literature available that highlights the gendered nature of space, many studies suggesting that domestic space is female while public or civic space is male (Low and Lawrence-Zúñiga 2003: 129–84, McDannell 1995). By relating encounters with the non-empirical to the domestic sphere, am I not immediately associating them with a female space and so suggesting that these spaces are specifically for women? There were no accounts from the data we have collected of men communing with the dead at the office or in other 'public' spaces. This kind of civic space is simply not seen as appropriate for this kind of behaviour. It is arguable that in the two contexts where the space in question is that of the church, a public or civic space, then the attempt to reconstruct this as a 'place' actually involves the 'domestication' of that space. In the case of the woman from inner-city Birmingham, it was while she was cleaning the sanctuary that the space became her 'place' for an encounter with the non-empirical (Schofield 1999). In the case of the Methodists, the place was created by filling the space with the memories of dead family members (Braddy 2002). In both cases we can see a domestication of the space involved.

This issue has to do with the way in which I constructed 'space' and 'place' in Chapter Four. By observing women involved in the practice of chatting with God or the dead, I constructed the activity as being both intimate and also set apart from the chaos of ordinary life. In doing this it is arguable that I have inevitably constructed the sacred in terms of the domestic. If we had observed other kinds of people doing other 'sacred' things then we may have arrived at a different series of definitions. It is worth looking again at the question of the 'domestic' or the 'intimate' in relation to gender before moving on to the wider questions at the end of this chapter.

In their book based on the study of religion in Kendal, Paul Heelas and Linda Woodhead ask why what they call the 'holistic milieu' is so dominated by women (2005: 94–107). The 'holistic milieu' is the part of contemporary religious practice that exists outside the mainstream congregations and includes various forms of healing practices, pagan and wiccan religions and other elements of what used to be called the 'New Age'. As we have seen, according to Heelas and Woodhead over 80 per cent of those involved in the holistic milieu in Kendal during their study were women (94). As they argue that the growth of the holistic milieu in recent years has been the result of what they call the subjective turn in society, and as that subjective turn (a concern primarily for the self and for self-fulfilment) has been shown by others to be equally true for men and women, Heelas and Woodhead were left with a problem in explaining the preponderance of women in holistic milieu practices (94–5).

They find their solution to this problem by dividing the subjective turn into two distinct movements, which they label 'individuated subjectivism' and 'relational subjectivism' (96). It is relational subjectivism, they argue, that is more common among women, and it is relational subjectivism that underpins the practices of the holistic milieu. I will come back to the idea of the subjective turn in my final chapter, and what I wish to highlight here is the relationship between women and relationality. Heelas and Woodhead go on to provide a significant amount of data showing that there is a statistical association between relationality and women, with women in particular being drawn to situations and practices where relationality is important (98–102).

What is interesting about the data we have collected, which forms the basis for the studies in the previous three chapters, is that as with Heelas and Woodhead's holistic milieu, relationality plays a very significant part. In the case of the small groups discussing death, or the young mothers talking about their stars, this is obvious and can be clearly demonstrated. In the case of the women who sit alone in the kitchen with a cup of tea, visit the grave of a loved one, or work alone while cleaning the church, the idea of relationality may seem more problematic. The point in each of these cases, however, is the nature of the relationship that they are having, at these times, with the non-empirical, that is with the dead or with God. I stated in Chapter Four that this relationship was 'intimate' and of the kind that Heelas and Woodhead demonstrate is particularly important to women. It is in the intimacy of the relationship with the non-empirical in these situations, therefore, that a specifically 'women's approach' to religion may be found.

When we bring this analysis into association with Robert Wuthnow's study of small groups we can see the next step in the discussion. Wuthnow argues that it is the intimate nature of the small groups themselves that leads to what he describes as the domestication of the sacred (1994: 255, 266). The members of the group build up an image of a God who is interested in exactly the same kind of concerns as they are themselves, that is the small, commonplace, domestic issues of everyday life. There is, therefore, a clear link between 'intimacy', 'relationality' and 'domesticity' and, it might be assumed, all three are closely associated with women. This would be fine except that the small groups Wuthnow is discussing are not dominated by women, and he refuses to recognize the phenomena he describes as specifically a woman's approach to religion. Given that we did not set out to observe men engaging intimately with the non-empirical, we actually have no data to suggest whether they do or not. We can only state that our evidence involves women. We are therefore back at our starting point. We need another way of looking at the issues.

## Conclusion: A Gendered Approach to Religion?

If we are still unable to claim that the relational and intimate, and the domestication of sacred space, are specific to women, then we have to move on to look at the issues raised in Chapter Five, more specifically at the idea that 'coping religion' could be specific to women. There is a significant and growing literature that explores the possibility and the shape of women's spirituality (King 1993, Woodhead 2002). There is a great deal in common between the information presented in this literature and the structure for 'coping religion' as identified in the present text (Ozorak 1996). The relationship that I outlined between coping religion and Womanist theology could bear this out. The question, however, is whether this 'coping religion' is specific to women, or whether it is coincidental that the evidence we have discovered has related to women, and that the kind of religion we have described may well have a wider constituency both in England and elsewhere.

In trying to provide an answer to this I want to begin by taking a sideways step and looking at the other significant feature of the people who have been the subject of our studies. These are not only women; they are women of a particular social class or status. Most of the women who populate the pages of Chapters Three, Four and Five are women from the lower social classes. They are not professionals, they are not well off, and they are not pursuing high-powered careers or engaged in higher education. The women we have observed are primarily single mothers; they are poor, not well educated and living in more or less desperate situations. The women interviewed by Sarah Schofield in Birmingham (Schofield 1999), the women I worked with in Manchester, the women whom Geoff Kimber listened to in North Warwickshire (Kimber 2001) are all traditional working-class women. Most were single parents, many were on benefits and all were within the lowest sector of society in terms of income and job prospects. Many of these women were also victims of social and domestic violence, lived in rough areas and were under constant threat of vandalism and abuse. They had it tough.

Throughout my analysis in Chapter Five I made a great deal of the tough life lived by the women in the various studies. It is this toughness, I would argue, and the attempts by these women to respond to the uncertainty and deprivation imposed by such an environment, that initially led me to coin the term 'coping religion'. These are women who need basic levels of support in order to 'cope' from day to day. They cannot rely on social services, the health service or traditional religion and so they turn to the dead, to spiritualism and to astrology. Does this mean, therefore, that what I have been describing is in fact the religion of a particular class of women, those who have nowhere else to turn, and that women of a higher status and men who can cope with life in general, do not need this kind of religion? That if they are not working-class women it has little relevance to them?

To some extent this must be true. However, as we have seen in the statistics relating to astrology and other practices, this is not the whole story. None of the phenomena that we have been considering are confined entirely to women from the poorer strata of our society. Astrology, spiritualism and visiting graveyards are all practised by women from a wide cross-section of society, and by a significant number of men as well. Women from the working classes may predominate, but they do not provide the entire constituency. There may be times when even the most educated, sophisticated and well-employed woman, or man for that matter, needs to 'cope' with life as they face it. At these times they may also turn to the kind of religious activities that we have been looking at, and this could be true even of those who maintain a regular relationship with one of the more traditional religions.

Gordon Lynch, a colleague at Birmingham University, along with a number of his research students, has been looking at the idea that 'raves' may perform a religious function for some of those who attend (Lynch 2005). While they have been unable to find anything in the way those who attend raves approach or talk about the experience that could traditionally be seen as 'religious', or even 'spiritual' (Beck 2005), they have noted that many of those who participate do so in order to enable them to cope with their everyday lives in difficult and stressful jobs. It is the ability to get out on a Saturday night and to completely unwind, even to lose control for a short time, that re-energizes many of those involved, so that they go back to their desks on Monday morning for another week of international financial dealing

or whatever they do. At this level, even if in no other way, the rave
provides a coping mechanism for these people and can be seen as part
of a 'coping religion'.

One of the difficulties of learning about the religious practices and
discourses of men, especially those from the same kind of areas as the
women we have been considering, is that they are so difficult to find
and engage with. Beatrix Campbell in her study of men from inner-
urban estates makes the point emphatically that the men are difficult
to find, and extremely difficult to talk to (Campbell 1993). She per-
sisted however, and found that the men also had rituals and practices
that helped them to cope with the stresses and strains of living in their
difficult environments. These rituals, however, involved stealing cars,
vandalizing property and other forms of anti-social behaviour. Apart
from their boredom and the lack of formal outlets for aggression, these
kinds of activities, according to Campbell, also enabled the men to deal
with the challenge to their understanding of masculinity, which had
become a serious problem on such estates. The need to find some
means of coping – in Campbell's analysis a 'displacement activity' – was
still necessary but it is clear that in this case, as with the example of the
raves, the kind of coping mechanisms engaged in do not involve the
non-empirical and so should not, therefore, form part of this particular
analysis.

Another factor to mention, as I draw this chapter to a close, is the
possibility that it is in fact working-class women who are most likely to
own up to holding the kind of beliefs, and partaking in the kind of
rituals, that we have been discussing. Even with ethnographic methods,
and the level of trust that is necessary for the informant to 'open up'
over a considerable period, it has never been easy for the student
researchers represented in this book to reveal the kind of religious
activity we have highlighted. It is not surface behaviour. It is not
something that people, even working-class women, talk about easily. It
is something very private and personal that only comes to light through
the long-term work of the ethnographer. Perhaps we have simply not
listened long and hard enough to other kinds of people, so that
practices and beliefs remain even more deeply hidden in these communities. Some evidence from other studies I have quoted highlights
the role of men, and the phenomena we have explored may not be as

restricted to working class women as our own evidence suggests. This implies that there is still a great deal of work to be done, and that as researchers we need to go out and find the men, the middle-class populations and the minority ethnic groups, to gain the trust of individuals and discover what they are doing in their own 'religious life'.

Looked at another way, it may be that in British society working-class single mothers most need the support of coping religions, and that large sections of our society never need such strategies or, as we have seen, find other ways of coping. In many other societies, especially those outside Europe and the United States, a much higher proportion of the population lives with constant uncertainty, poverty and illness. We would expect to see in these situations a much wider take-up of 'coping religions' of many different kinds. Our evidence suggests that this is clearly the case. This indicates that the kind of beliefs and practices that we have been discussing provide the basis for all religion, wherever in the world it may be found; this is the topic of my final chapter.

# Chapter 7

# On the Elementary Form of Religious Life

When Emile Durkheim set out to discover and elucidate the 'elementary forms of religious life' his first instinct was to turn to the religious life of people very different from those of his contemporary France (Durkheim 1995). France, Durkheim knew, was a civilized and sophisticated society. Surely there was no possibility that elementary forms of anything would be found at such a pinnacle of social evolution. Durkheim therefore turned to what he assumed was the simplest and 'most primitive' form of society available to him in order to discover religion at its most basic (1).

Unfortunately, as is well known in anthropological and sociological circles, Durkheim made a number of fundamental errors in the realization of this project (Morris 1987: 106–22). The society he chose, that of the Arrernte of Central Australia, was not as simple and unsophisticated as he had thought (Morphy 1998). It has also been shown that there is no clear relationship between the simplicity of social organization – the marker Durkheim used to measure the level of sophistication (1995: 1) – and the complexity of intellectual culture (Sahlins 1974: 38). And, ultimately, even the best data available to him on Australian societies was itself seriously flawed (Morphy 1998: 18–20).

There was one more major error that meant Durkheim would never find the 'elementary' forms of religious life halfway around the world in a completely 'other' society. He assumed a one-to-one relationship between society and religion. The people of Central Australia formed one society and, Durkheim assumed, they had one religion, the religion of that people. The same should have been true of contemporary France, although it clearly was not. Durkheim himself came from a Jewish family (Fields 1995: xxix–xxx) and even if we assume that the primary religion of France at the end of the nineteenth century was

Catholicism, the presence of Jews, the impact of various Protestant groups and the revolutionary legacy of anti-clericalism and atheism meant there was no single religion that could plausibly be identified as 'the religion' of France. France could be seen as a corruption of the pristine state of the native, native Australian, and the notion of the 'noble savage' lies behind this distinction. However, religious diversity in France suggests that there might also have been a variety of religious discourses in Australian societies – and arguably more variety of religious discourse in France than Durkheim or any other sociologist before the 1960s would acknowledge.

Where I would follow Durkheim, unlike perhaps most ethnographers, is in the idea of the search for an 'elementary form' of religion, or religious life (Fields 1995: lix–lxi). In the introduction to this book I raised the issue of the definitions of religion, and argued that too many contemporary definitions take Christianity as their model and assume that all other religious practices, religious discourses or religious lives must contain the same elements as the Christian. This – as I hope I have shown in the main text – is simply not the case, at least as far as systematization, transcendence and transformation are concerned. There are forms of religious activity in Britain today that do not follow the Christian model. What I am not saying, however, is that all other forms of religion must be modelled on the religious practices and discourses I have outlined in this book. I am not seeking an all-encompassing, definitive definition of religion.

I want to suggest that the kind of religion, the particular form of engagement with the non-empirical, that I have been outlining can in some way be understood as the most 'elementary' or 'elemental' form of religion, the ground upon which all other forms are built (Fields 1995: lx). I do not mean that the form of religion I have outlined can be proven to be the earliest form of religion in an evolutionary cycle (although I might, in a different context, want to theorize that it was). Nor am I suggesting that the form of religion I have presented is necessarily the simplest or least sophisticated form (although once again that may be the case, depending on how we define 'simple' and 'sophisticated'). What I am suggesting, by defining this form of religion as 'elementary', is that it is probably the most widespread and most common form of religion, the form of religion to which human beings revert when all other forms collapse.

These are big claims, which I cannot fully justify in my final chapter. I want to explore them, through the analysis of various other authors, and present them so that they can be tested by others.

## Defining the form of religion

When others have approached the kind of data I have presented in this book they have used labels such as 'popular religion', 'folk religion' or 'implicit religion' as defining terms. Each of these, however, refers to something different and only 'popular religion' comes close to identifying the area I have tried to explore.

'Folk religion', for example, refers to a semi-pagan religious discourse in which certain rituals and non-empirical entities inhabit the religious world (Clark 1982). I am not trying to define a religious discourse as such, but the principles I have outlined – situational belief, the imminence of the non-empirical, coping religions – could be found in various religious discourses, including Christian discourses, as Sarah Schofield's analysis has shown (Schofield 1999). What I am describing, therefore, is not 'folk religion', although a folk religion that speaks of fairies, popular superstitions, sprites and other traditional non-empirical entities would probably function in a similar way. It is only when 'specialists' start to construct grand theories of fairyland, with different sprites and their actions in the world, that the form of religion changes into something very different.

The term 'implicit religion' also fails to capture exactly what I have been exploring in this text. This is a term coined by Edward Bailey (1998) to describe situations where the functions of religion have been taken on by other institutions in society. For example, the pub can act as a meeting place and a place for moral discussion within a particular community, and can be seen as implicitly religious for those who attend regularly. More commonly, the cult of celebrity or the ritual surrounding football have been seen by commentators as taking over the role of religion in contemporary society. All these kinds of analysis, however, have placed the argument the wrong way up. They have begun with a definition of religion – generally based on the Christian model outlined in Chapter One – and then, seeing that the numbers of those who practise traditional religions have declined dramatically, sought other contexts in which something that looks like the pre-defined religion is taking place. This is not a sensible way of theorizing about religion. I have, in this text, suggested a couple of contexts where coping mechanisms are used that do not interact with the non-empirical, specifically in the case of raves and of inner-urban male violence. However, I would not identify either of these as implicitly religious: they are simply alternative ways of coping, alongside that which I am defining as 'religious'.

Another discourse that has emerged in recent years, to widen the scope of the 'religious' in contemporary Western societies, focuses on 'spirituality' (McGuire 1997). Most who write about spirituality warn that, like religion, it is impossible to define. The term has come to fill a presumed gap where the word 'religion' no longer appears totally appropriate. Spirituality has a sense of the individualistic about it, as opposed to the communal nature of 'religion'. It is also introspective and subjective. It is about the individual's own series of existential questions, or the individual's own engagement with the divine. Spirituality is well described in Paul Heelas and Linda Woodhead's (2005) work on wellbeing and the subjective trend in our society. Whatever the implications of such a trend, which I will come back to later, it is clear that what Heelas, Woodhead and others refer to as 'spirituality' is not related to the kind of coping religions I have been describing in this text.

Finally, I need to note Forster's (1995) reference to 'residual religions', not because I think this is a better term for what I am exploring than 'popular', 'folk' or 'implicit' religions, but simply that in choosing the term 'residual' Forster has highlighted the main reason why other terms do not work. These terms are all still rooted in the Christian definition of 'religion', except that in these cases what the scholar is investigating is what is thought to be left over – the residual element – by removing 'real religion' from the frame. This is fundamentally flawed. Far from coping religions and related phenomena being 'residual', they are 'fundamental' or, in Durkheim's language, 'elementary'.

## A Tylorian Reconstruction

Most of this chapter has been negative, specifying what the kind of religion I have been discussing is not. We now have to begin the process of reconstruction. If this form of religion is not 'popular', 'implicit', 'residual', or even identifiable with 'spirituality', then what is it, and how can we theorize its relationship to other forms of religion? In order to do this I want to turn to Edward Tylor's discussion of religion in his 1871 work *Primitive Culture*.

I want to consider the argument by which Tylor constructs his model of religion, by a logical progression from simple ideas to complex issues. Stanley Tambiah describes Tylor's 'scientific method' as 'the sorting of phenomena into "species"-like grouping, and then arranging these species in levels or grades' (1990: 44). A number of other authors have commented on the sheer amount of data quoted in Tylor's work. Robert Lowie, for example, says that in 'turning from the psychological to the chronological aspects of Tylor's scheme, I must confess that it is not in all details perfectly clear to me, for the overwhelming mass of concrete illustrations is leavened by a minimum of logical correlation' (1936: 118). Louis Jordan complains that Tylor's argument is actually too complicated to be true to nature (1905: 263). I would argue, however, that it is this very complexity, this overwhelming mass of concrete illustration, which allows us to rework Tylor's material in a new and interesting fashion.

At first sight Tylor's argument looks to be an evolutionary process, and he clearly understands it in this way. Each chapter, for example, or each argument within a chapter, begins with simple instances of a phenomenon, illustrated primarily by examples from 'savage societies'. Tylor then shows how the same principle develops through different layers to more complex forms, with illustrations of the higher or more complex phenomena taken primarily from 'civilized societies'. The whole structure is developmental, and is mapped onto a pre-conceived evolutionary model. One element of all these arguments, however, undermines their evolutionary framework, and this needs to be explored in more detail.

While Tylor uses examples from 'savage societies' in the earlier stages of his argument, and examples from 'civilized societies' in the later stages, the excess of data reveals anomalies. We find, for example, that ghosts are found in 'civilized' societies – usually seen by the uneducated, although not always, as with the Spiritualists – and that the idea of a 'High God' is present in many of the 'savage' societies.

In other words, while the form of the argument may suggest an evolutionary framework, the facts he presents, the concrete illustrations, undermine the central principle of this framework. For every phenomenon, there are examples from 'primitive societies', from 'barbarian societies', from 'civilised' and modern societies. The primary emphasis in each society may be on one particular element, whether ancestor worship, polytheism, nature spirits, or whatever. What is clear, however, is that all the other phenomena also appear to be present in the same society, even if only within subsections or at different levels, such as between the family and the wider political system.

In late Victorian Britain, for example, the religious norm was monotheistic ethical Christianity, but ancestor worship and polytheistic gods were also part of the picture, for example in the cult of the saints. Some people believed in ghosts and local nature spirits, and healing was understood in some parts of the country as the departing of spirits from the body (Davies 1999). All these religious elements existed together as part of a complex, if not coherent, whole. But by taking each element one at a time and positing a supposed progression between them, Tylor fails to notice the form of the complex whole that he is describing. This is as true of his so-called savage societies as it is for Victorian Britain. There may be ancestor cults, spirit beings, fetishes and High Gods all existing simultaneously in the Tylor account, but they are not connected in any continuous form.

If this is the case for Victorian Britain and for 'savage societies', then why should it not be the case for contemporary English society? What I have been outlining in this book, therefore, can be seen as simply one layer of the many different layers of religious practice that make up any normal society. That is uncontroversial. My more radical point is that the level of religion I have been exploring may well form the base layer of this wider structure, the foundation on which all others have been built. Tylor, talking in evolutionary terms, describes the base layer, the fundamental or elementary form of religion in his schema, as 'animism' (1871: I, 384–5). Is the phenomena I have been exploring in this book, therefore, simply the animistic layer of the wider contemporary English religious system?

## Discourse

As with the discussion on situational belief in the last chapter, I have offered a version of this analysis of Tylor's layered approach to religion in print on at least two previous occasions. In each case I suggested that what is layered, in my reworking of Tylor's analysis, can best be described by the word 'discourse'. But 'discourse' is subtly different in each case, and this has an effect on how the argument is understood.

In my original article on the reworking of Tylor's thesis (Stringer 1999b) I began my reconstruction of his ideas with a discussion of his work on language, which in his original volumes immediately precedes the analysis I have examined above. On the basis of this discussion of language I introduced the idea of 'discourse', arguing that Tylor sees religion, which he defines as the belief in spiritual beings, as 'a discourse, a way of talking about the world in which different rules apply ... it demands a switch of thought world, a switch which we still experience in poetry and which we can just about grasp, a switch which demands its own logic and its own rationality' (1999b: 549). In this I follow Dan Sperber (1974) and the analysis outlined in Chapter Three. Religion therefore is seen as a discourse, a way of speaking or thinking, which has the features specified by Sperber, that is it deals with those aspects of knowledge that cannot be handled by the empirical or encyclopedic approach. Discourse in this sense is a particular type of language that is not related directly to its content – except that the content is in some way non-empirical – but related rather to its inner logic or rationality. This understanding of discourse echoes Clifford Geertz's ideas of 'perspectives' within a culture, such that the historical, the scientific, the aesthetic, the common sense and the religious perspectives each deal with different aspects of reality that cannot easily be translated each into the other (1966: 26–8). Religion, therefore, is that body of discourse/language dealing specifically with the non-empirical.

In my second presentation of these ideas I was specifically interested in the place of popular traditions of worship and devotion in the late medieval period, and their relationship to the official liturgy and doctrine of the Church (2005: 163–5). Here I drew on Gerd Baumann's (1996) understanding of discourse, in which he outlines the possibility of a 'dominant discourse' and a 'demotic discourse' among particular populations, the former being held by those in authority while the latter is held by the ordinary people. The layers of Tylor's analysis in this concept are levels of demotic discourse held by different populations within a society, or by the same populations at different times and for different purposes. The King of Spain in the sixteenth century, for example, was able to use both dominant and demotic discourses on religion on different occasions (Christian 1981: 148–53).

The nature of discourse in this context is determined by content, structure and form, and dominant and demotic discourses could have been very similar; both deal clearly with the non-empirical, but one relates to local shrines and popular rituals, including the driving out of spirits and other lesser beings, while the other relies on the systematic definition of orthodoxy and the official liturgical engagement with God. In this analysis it is the content that defines the layers of discourse on the non-empirical present within society.

However, I want to reject both previous understandings of discourse and their implications. It is not a specific layer of discourse relating to the non-empirical that concerns me, nor do I think that the distinction between the layers of religious discourse is seen in terms of a difference in the content of the discourses involved. I want to use 'discourse' here as I do at the beginning of my book *Sociological History of Christian Worship* (2005: 17–23); that is, I want to talk about different religious discourses in terms of the different internal logic of those discourses, and their common content. We can therefore talk about a set of Christian discourses, a set of pagan discourses, a set of Islamic discourses, and so on. We could also talk about a series of astrological discourses, a series of discourses on the dead, including Spiritualism, a series of wellbeing discourses, and so on. The list is endless, and making clear distinctions is problematical since many such discourses are a combination of, for example, Christian and pagan, Christian and wellbeing, or astrological and Spiritualist. The point, however, is that within each of these overarching discourses it is still possible to engage with the non-empirical in a whole series of layers, as set out in Tylor's analysis. Or, to put it another way, each layer can be expressed in a wide range of different discourses.

So, to return to the present analysis, I am proposing that the kind of religious response I have been highlighting represents the base layer of Tylor's construction, the most elementary form of religious response. That can be expressed, as with the woman in Sarah Schofield's (1999) analysis, within a basically Christian discourse or, as with the women in the parent and toddler group, through a discourse of astrology or Spiritualism. It is the form of religious response that I am highlighting in this analysis, not the content. We could call this a particular religious 'grammar', although I would prefer to keep that term for expressing structural elements within a specific discourse. We could also refer to these layers as 'genres', following a literary model (Fairclough 2003: 65–86). In this case the 'coping genre' could theoretically be expressed in a range of distinct religious discourses, in the same way that you could have a feminist detective story, a post-modern detective story or, conceivably, a Christian or Spiritualist detective story (Denzin 1997: 163–98). The exact term, however, may not be relevant at this stage in the argument.


## Animism


This discussion has already raised the question of whether there is any resemblance between what I have described as the base layer of Tylor's reconstructed schema, and what Tylor himself refers to as 'animism'. It is well known that Tylor understood 'animism' to be the most basic form of religion upon which all other forms are built. What is not so well known is what Tylor meant by the term (Stringer 1999b, Harvey 2005: 5–9). It is usually assumed that he meant, and what the term has come to mean generally, is that primitive people understood all material things to have souls and that they engaged with other objects as if they were human. This is not the case at all. Tylor is not really talking about 'souls' in any specific sense. He is essentially arguing that there is a non-empirical element, a 'spiritual' part, to people and to many other objects in the world, and that some non-empirical elements exist as disembodied entities or forces. In other words all people engage with that which is non-empirical, but what they understand as the specific form of the non-empirical may vary from society to society (Stringer 1999b: 549). At this level, what Tylor is referring to as 'animism' and what I am presenting here are not very different. It may be possible to call the layer, or genre, of religion I am highlighting 'animistic', although given the many other associations for this word, I would be reluctant to do this (Harvey 2005).

In relating the concepts of this book to Tylor's understanding of animism, however I must entirely reject two elements of his thesis. The religious approach I am describing is not seen as evolutionary, nor am I offering any psychological speculation about its origin or current practice. Like Tylor, I am simply suggesting that the evidence points to a common structure or genre of religion that might be termed 'animism' (Stringer 1999b: 543).

What I can do, therefore, is to identify more clearly the base layer of the religious structure. I have highlighted three elements in this text: the situational, unsystematic nature of belief; an intimate association with the non-empirical; and an attempt to respond to pragmatic questions concerned with daily life and coping with everyday problems. Is there enough here for a universal definition of religion?

Of the three elements I have highlighted, it is the intimate relationship with the non-empirical that relates my ideas most closely to contemporary thinking on animism (Harvey 2005: 196–7). Essentially, the individual relates to the non-empirical in the same way as to another human person. Graham Harvey, in his recent analysis of animism, uses Irving Hallowell's terminology to refer to the non-empirical other as 'other-than-human persons', so stressing the intimate nature of the relations (2005: 17–20, Hallowell 1960). It is assumed that the non-empirical entity, or other-than-human person, can hear, understand and in some circumstances act on what is being said. There is no explicit sense, however, within the fieldwork presented here that the non-empirical can respond, talk or take significant action in the world, although that may be different in other contexts. The exact form of the non-empirical other in any particular circumstances depends on the specific religious discourse in which the individual is participating, but the main point is the level of intimacy and, derived from that, the level of concern and care expected from the other that is most important. It is because the non-empirical other is thought to care about the little, day- to-day problems of the individual's life that the other is turned to regularly. Hence the 'caring' and 'coping' relationship with the other allows us to identify it with the animistic genre.

The first element, the situational – non-systematic – nature of belief in the other, also relates to the pragmatic coping nature of the religious approach. Individuals will turn to non-empirical others, or other-than-human persons, who can in some way or other 'work', who can make a difference. If chatting to gran at her grave or consulting the stars or even engaging in conversations with God no longer provided the comfort and strength to carry on, then they would be rejected. No more understanding of these different phenomena is required than is needed to understand the action itself. These individuals do not have to construct grand theories of the nature of life after death to know that gran is still with them and looking after them. They do not need to understand the detailed interaction of the stars to gain comfort from what the astrologer says. It is others who choose, for other purposes, to construct entire theological systems or to build powerful, and often power-hungry, institutions to control the other. For the ordinary individual it is the day-to-day interaction at an intimate level, in order to deal with serious pragmatic problems, that forms the basis for this elementary form of religion.

## Secularization

The most common framework for understanding religion in contemporary Britain is that of secularization (Bruce 2002, Davie 1994). This understanding emerges from the traditional definition of religion highlighted in Chapter One. Those who study the role of religion in contemporary English society agree that, within a traditional definition of religion, practice and perhaps also belief have been declining for over a century (Davie 1987, 41–4). Mainstream church attendance has been going down steadily, although the rate varies from church to church, and over the last thirty years or so it is also possible to detect a decline in belief in God and other formal non-empirical notions

(Bruce 1995: 15–18). Beyond this, however, scholars differ as to the nature and importance of secularization.

There are essentially two schools of thought. Some see attendance at churches and mosques as the principle form of religious expression, and therefore see the decline in numbers as a sign of real decline in religious inclination among the general population (Bruce 2002). Others suggest that attendance at formal, institutional religious gatherings is only one aspect of religiosity in Britain, and argue that the religious landscape of Britain is changing rather than declining (Davie 1994, Heelas and Woodhead 2005). My own understanding, based on the analysis in this book, is closer to the latter position. However, I am not sure that there is a new form of religious expression in Britain today, and I would suggest that the form of religion I have been exploring has always been present; but we have not sought it, and have therefore never really seen it.

At one level this is simply a question of 'discourse'. As long as Christianity formed the dominant religious discourse in Britain, the religious approach I have highlighted would have been expressed in Christian terms. The 'intimate other' would have been saints, or guardian angels, or even Jesus, 'our friend and brother'. The unsystematic nature of the belief statements would have been hidden because most of the belief statements drawn on would have come from within the Christian tradition, but the basic coping structure of the religious genre would have been much as I have explained it in this text. Such a distinctive religious approach would hardly have been noticed, except by those who felt that this was only 'nominal' Christianity, or some kind of 'folk' Christianity, or merely 'superstition' (Williams 1999).

If such was the case, then the decline of Christianity as the dominant religious discourse has only made this kind of religiosity more visible as people have turned to other discourses within which to express it. The situational nature of the belief statements becomes more obvious when Christian ideas of death are merged with those from other traditions, and when the non-empirical is experienced primarily in the form of dead relatives rather than through Christian figures (Ahern 1987). Secularization, therefore, has revealed this layer of religiosity rather than caused it. Indeed, this layer has always existed and what we see now is not something new but a continuation of a fundamentally human process found in all societies.

When we look more closely, however, it is clear that the animistic layer of religious practice has not always been expressed in Christian terms, even when Christianity was the dominant religious discourse in England. The evidence of many folk beliefs and practices throughout the Victorian and Edwardian periods can be easily framed within an animistic genre (Davies 1999, Williams 1999). What is interesting, however, is how these beliefs and practices have themselves changed over the centuries, as the discourses associated with this form of religion have mutated.

Owen Davies, in *Witchcraft, Magic and Culture 1736–1951* (1999), tells us that in the Victorian era many popular beliefs were rooted in the local traditions and landscapes of the country (167–213). They were concerned with witchcraft, small non-empirical beings such as fairies and goblins, and other kinds of spirit. There were men and women – 'cunning folk' – who specialized in controlling the non-empirical through magical formulas and the use of herbs. Some healers travelled around the country selling their skills and wares, while others were trained locally and lived in rural communities (214–28). As urbanism developed these activities changed subtly, with more focus on the traveller and the Romany whose traditions were represented at fairs and markets (258–65). The local healer, with their particular lore and connection with specific non-empirical beings, began to fall out of fashion and mutate into children's story characters. Later, astrology and spiritualism began to emerge in urban settings, building on earlier traditions but now with a semi-professional, semi-scientific approach to meet the needs of the wider society (266–70).

Now we see another subtle shift. Local healers have all but died out, and the Romany traditions are marginal. In the late twentieth and early twenty-first centuries sprites and goblins, fairies and pixies have no significant place in English religious discourses. Saints and angels have some hold, but are not really significant (Heathcote-James 2001). It is the dead, and almost always the friendly dead, who have come to fill the role of the intimate non-empirical other, and new forms of healing and fortune-telling are meeting the need for coping traditions. The animistic genre of religion may not be declining in the context of so-called 'secularization', but there is no doubt that it is transforming itself to meet contemporary requirements.

What, then, should we make of Paul Heelas and Linda Woodhead's contention that contemporary religion has been affected by what they, following Charles Taylor, describe as the 'subjective turn' (2005: 2–5, Taylor 1991: 26)? In many ways this does not affect my analysis. If we look at what is claimed for the 'subjective turn' in society (Heelas and Woodhead 2005: 1–11), it is clear that it represents a change of dominant discourse, without necessarily changing the nature of religious practice in society. Heelas and Woodhead describe a limited range of changes to practice – what they call the rise of the 'holistic milieu' – which the change in discourse can be seen to have influenced (94–110). There has been a move away from traditional Christian or congregational contexts to those defined by wellbeing and personal development.

The subjective turn has also influenced the discourse of Christianity, leading to different practices in some traditional contexts (124–5). None of this, however, affects my analysis directly because in their study of Kendal, the Lancaster University team were not looking for the religious genre I have been describing, and had no way of recognizing it. They assumed that religious commitment could most easily be measured in associational contexts, either in traditional institutions such as churches – the 'congregational domain' – or in new institutions such as clinics and community groups – the 'holistic milieu' (12–13). They did not look for the personal, unsystematic, intimate relations with the 'other' that we have observed in this book.

It is arguable that the current trend towards seeing the closely-related dead as the most common form of non-empirical other engaged with, is directly related to the subjective turn in the dominant discourses of society. It is possible to see such dead relatives as in some ways an extension of the self and the conversations held with these others as being self-obsessed, or at least self-focused. My evidence from Manchester, however, would not support this, since the women I was listening to talking about astrology and spiritualism were usually seeking help with practical problems to do with their children and their children's health, rather than their own personal issues. But this may be, as I suggested in the previous chapter, primarily a class issue, and if we looked at how professional women relate to astrology and the issues they bring to their conversations with the dead, then we might well see a much more subjective approach.

Religion, therefore, is changing in contemporary Britain; or rather, the dominant religious discourses are changing, and that affects the layers of Tylor's model. The base, however – the elementary, 'animistic' form of religion – arguably remains constant in its 'form', in how it fundamentally works, while it adapts constantly to the dominant discourses around it.

## Conclusion

In this work I have tried to present a different way of looking at religion. Much of the evidence is not new, although some of the practices revealed among ordinary English people have surprised many who have seen this material. The structure or 'genre' of religion that I have presented in this final chapter is not original: Tylor described something similar as his 'animistic layer'. Other writers on animism have recognized a similar structure of religion in many different parts of the world (Harvey 2005). It is not usual to describe the basic religious attitude of most British people as 'animistic', but if we substitute the word 'superstitious' we can see that other commentators have made a similar proposition. This animistic genre of religion may be dismissed as 'superstition' or damned with faint praise as 'popular', 'implicit' or 'residual'; it may be treated as a lesser form of religion when measured against accepted definitions based on a Christian model. I suggest, however, that it is the 'elementary' or primary form of religion upon which all other forms of religion are built.

This thesis may not change our understanding of religion in contemporary Britain, but I hope that it will add a layer of sophistication to the analysis of those such as Steve Bruce, Grace Davie, Paul Heelas and Linda Woodhead who have not recognized its importance. I hope this analysis will change the way in which we talk and think about religion. I want to offer a new definition of it that is rooted in people's unsystematic use of belief statements, their intimate relationships with the non-empirical other, and their need to cope pragmatically with everyday problems.

This is not to deny that the major world religions with their sophisticated systematic theologies, their transcendent gods and their salvific aims, are not significant, or that many people take them very seriously. But I am suggesting that these forms of religion are aberrations, the form of religion generally accepted only by a small minority, even when they form the basis of the dominant religious discourse in society. There may be other contexts, as with the rise of Islamic traditions at present, where people turn to these religions and their discourses for other purposes (Asad 1993). When it 'comes to the crunch', however, with ordinary people living their ordinary lives and coping with all their troubles, they will resort to an animistic religious genre, even if it is expressed within the discourse of a world religion or in terms of a subjective contemporary spirituality.

The questions that remain are not to do with the animistic genre as such, although I would hope that careful listening in further ethnographic work will help us to understand it better. The questions that remain concern the exceptions rather than the rule. Why do people construct religious systems and build religious institutions? How does the development of other genres of religious practice relate to different social contexts – perhaps a Weberian analysis is possible here – and how are genres of religious practice related to the distribution and maintenance of power in a society? What happens when an individual experiences the transcendent – an altered state of consciousness or a mystical vision – and how does this affect the animistic genre? How does the animistic genre of the majority relate to the ethical implications of complex religious discourses? The list could continue, and all these questions are beyond the scope of this work. My aim here is simply to offer the evidence needed to invert the current model of religion, to turn over the definitional stone, and to examine the questions that emerge.

# Bibliography

Agar, M. H. (1980), *The Professional Stranger: An Informal Introduction to Ethnography*. San Diego: Academic Press.

Ahern, G. (1987), "'I do believe in Christmas": white working-class people and Anglican clergy in inner-city London', in G. Ahern and G. Davie, *Inner City God: The Nature of Belief in the Inner City*. London: Hodder & Stoughton, 77–133.

Alasuutari, P. (1995), *Researching Culture: Qualitative Methods and Cultural Studies*. London: Sage Publications.

Arnal, W. A. (2000), 'Definition', in W. Braun and R. T. McCutcheon (eds), *Guide to the Study of Religion*. London: Cassell, 21–34.

Asad, T. (ed.) (1973), *Anthropology and the Colonial Encounter*. London: Ithaca Press.

Asad, T. (1993), *Genealogies of Religion: Discipline and Reasons of Power in Christianity and Islam*. Baltimore: Johns Hopkins University Press.

Bailey, E. (1998), *Implicit Religion: An Introduction*. London: Middlesex University Press.

Barth, F. (1975), *Ritual and Knowledge among the Baktaman of New Guinea*. Oslo: Universitetsforlaget.

Baumann, G. (1996), *Contesting Culture: Discourses of Identity in Multi-Ethnic London*. Cambridge: University of Cambridge Press.

Beattie, J. (1964), *Other Cultures: Aims, Methods and Achievements in Social Anthropology*. London: Routledge and Kegan Paul.

Beck, G. D. (2005), 'Post-rave spirituality: an ethnographic analysis and evangelical theological engagement with the conscious partying movement'. Unpublished MPhil thesis, University of Birmingham.

Belmont, N. (1982), 'Superstition and popular religion in Western societies', in M. Izard and P. Smith (eds), *Between Belief and Transgression*. Chicago: University of Chicago Press, 9–23.

Berger, P. L. and Luckmann, T. (1966), *The Social Construction of Reality*. Harmondsworth: Penguin Books.

Blackmore, S. and Seebold, M. (2000), 'The effect of horoscopes on women's relations', *Correlation*, 19, (2), 14–23.

Boissevain, J. (1980), *A Village in Malta, Fieldwork Edition*. New York: Holt, Reinhart and Winston.

Braddy, M. L. (2002), 'Religion and faith in a Norfolk village'. Unpublished PhD thesis, University of Birmingham.

Braun, W. (2000), 'Religion' in W. Braun and R. T. McCutcheon (eds), *Guide to the Study of Religion*. London: Cassell, 3–18.

Brown, C. G. (2001), *The Death of Christian Britain: Understanding Secularisation 1800–2000*. London: Routledge.

Bruce, S. (1995), *Religion in Modern Britain*. Oxford: Oxford University Press.

Bruce, S. (2002), *God is Dead: Secularization in the West*. Oxford: Blackwell.

Campbell, B. (1993), *Goliath: Britain's Dangerous Places*. London: Methuen.

Capps, W. H. (1995), *Religious Studies: The Making of a Discipline*. Minneapolis: Fortress Press.

Chidester, D. and Linenthal, E. T. (1995), 'Introduction', in D. Chidester and E. T. Linenthal (eds), *American Sacred Space*. Bloomington: Indiana University Press.

Christian, W. A. (1981), *Local Religion in Sixteenth-Century Spain*. Princeton: Princeton University Press.

Clark, D. (1982), *Between Pulpit and Pew: Folk Religion in a North Yorkshire Fishing Village*. Cambridge: Cambridge University Press.

Clifford, J. and Marcus, G. F. (eds) (1986), *Writing Culture: The Poetics and Politics of Ethnography*. Berkley: University of California Press.

Cole, D. (1983), '"The value of a person lies in his *herzensbildung*": Franz Boaz' Baffin Island letter-diary, 1883–1884', in G. W. Stocking (ed.), *Observers Observed: Essays on Ethnographic Fieldwork*. Madison: University of Wisconsin Press, 13–52.

Connolly, P. (1999), 'Introduction', in P. Connolly (ed.) *Approaches to the Study of Religion*. London: Cassell, 1–9.

D'Aeth, L. J. H. (1999), 'Can soap opera care for its audience?' Unpublished PhD thesis, University of Birmingham.

Davie, G. (1987), 'The nature of belief in the inner city', in G. Ahern and G. Davie, *Inner City God: The Nature of Belief in the Inner City*. London: Hodder & Stoughton, 21–76.

Davie, G. (1994), *Religion in Britain since 1945: Believing without Belonging*. Oxford: Blackwell.

Davies, C. A. (1999), *Reflexive Ethnography: A Guide to Researching Selves and Others*. London: Routledge.

Davies, O. (1999), *Witchcraft, Magic and Culture 1736–1951*. Manchester: Manchester University Press.

Day, A. F. (2006), 'Believing in belonging in contemporary Britain: a case study from Yorkshire'. Unpublished PhD thesis, Lancaster University.

Denzin, N. K. (1997), *Interpretive Ethnography: Ethnographic Practices for the Twenty-First Century*. London: Sage.

Dubuisson, D. (2003), *The Western Construction of Religion: Myths, Knowledge and Ideology*. Baltimore: Johns Hopkins University Press.

Durkheim, E. (1995), *The Elementary Forms of Religious Life*. New York: The Free Press.

Evans-Pritchard, E. E. (1940), *The Nuer: A Description of the Modes of Livelihood and Political Institutions of a Nilotic People*. Oxford: Oxford University Press.

Evans-Pritchard, E. E. (1951), *Kinship and Marriage among the Nuer*. Oxford: Oxford University Press.

Evans-Pritchard, E. E. (1956), *Nuer Religion*. Oxford: Oxford University Press.

Evans-Pritchard, E. E. (1965), *Theories of Primitive Religion*. Oxford: Oxford University Press.

Fairclough, N. (2003), *Analysing Discourse: Textual Analysis for Social Research*. London: Routledge.

Favret-Saada, J. (1980), *Deadly Words: Witchcraft in the Bocage*. Cambridge: Cambridge University Press.

Fields, K. E. (1995), 'Translator's introduction: religion as an eminently social thing', in E. Durkheim, *The Elementary Forms of Religious Life*. New York: The Free Press, xvii–lxxiii.

Forster, P. G. (1995), 'Residual religiosity on a Hull council estate', in P. G. Forster (ed.), *Contemporary Mainstream Religion: Studies from Humberside and Lincolnshire*. Aldershot: Avebury, 1–33.

Geertz, C. (1966), 'Religion as a cultural system', in Michael Banton (ed.), *Anthropological Approaches to the Study of Religion*. London: Tavistock.

Geertz, C. (1975), *The Interpretation of Cultures*. London: Hutchinson.

Geertz, C. (1988), *Works and Lives: The Anthropologist as Author*. Stanford: Stanford University Press.

Gellner, D. N. (1999), 'Anthropological approaches', in P. Connolly (ed.), *Approaches to the Study of Religion*. London: Cassell, 10–41.

Grant, J. (1989), *White Women's Christ and Black Women's Jesus: Feminist Christology and Womanist Response*. Atlanta: Scholar's Press.

Gullestad, M. (1984), *Kitchen-Table Society: A Case Study of the Family Life and Friendships of Young Working-Class Mothers in Urban Norway*. Oslo: Universitetsforlaget.

Hallowell, A. I. (1960), 'Objiwa ontology, behaviour and world view', in S. Diamond (ed.), *Culture in History: Essays in Honour of Paul Radin*. Columbia University Press, 19–52.

Hammersley, M. (1992), *What's Wrong with Ethnography? Methodological Explorations*. London: Routledge.

Harvey, G. (2005), *Animism: Respecting the Living World*. London: Hurst & Co.

Hastrup, K. (1995), *A Passage to Anthropology: Between Experience and Theory*. London: Routledge.

Heathcote-James, E. (2001), *Seeing Angels*. London: John Blake Publishing.

Heathcote-James, E. (2003), *After-Death Communication*. London: Metro Publishing.

Heelas, P., Woodhead, L. with Seel, B., Szerszynski, B. and Tusting, K. (2005), *The Spiritual Revolution: Why Religion is giving Way to Spirituality*. Oxford: Blackwell.

Heim, S. M. (1995), *Salvations: Truth and Difference in Religion*. Maryknoll: Orbis Books.

Hervieu-Léger, D. (2000), *Religion as Chain of Memory*. Cambridge: Polity Press.

Hobson, D. (1980), 'Housewives and the mass media', in S. Hall, D. Hobson, A. Lowe and P. Willis (eds) *Culture, Media, Language*. London: Hutchinson.

Hobson, D. (1982), *Crossroads: The Drama of a Soap Opera.* London: Methuen.

Idowu, E. B. (1973), *African Traditional Religion: A Definition.* London: SCM Press.

Jordan, L. H. (1905), *Comparative Religion: Its Genesis and Growth.* Edinburgh: T & T. Clark.

Kimber, G. F. (2001), 'An investigation into the attitude of a Warwickshire mining community to church and spirituality'. Unpublished MPhil thesis, University of Birmingham.

King, U. (1993), *Women and Spirituality: Voices of Protest and Promise.* London: Macmillan.

Knott, K. (2005), *The Location of Religion: A Spatial Analysis.* London: Equinox.

Kuklick, H. (1991), *The Savage Within: The Social History of British Anthropology 1885–1945.* Cambridge: Cambridge University Press.

Kulick, D. and Willson, M. (eds) (1995), *Taboo, Sex, Identity and Erotic Subjectivity in Anthropological Fieldwork.* London: Routledge.

La Fontaine, J. S. (1985), *Initiation, Ritual Drama and Secret Knowledge Across the World.* Harmondsworth: Penguin.

Lane, B. C. (1988), *Landscapes of the Sacred: Geography and Narrative in American Spirituality.* New York: Paulist Press.

Lassiter, L. E. (ed.) (2005), *The Chicago Guide to Collaborative Ethnography.* Chicago: University of Chicago Press

Leach, E. R. (1966a), 'Rethinking anthropology', in *Rethinking Anthropology.* London: Athlone Press, 1–27.

Leach, E. R. (1966b), 'Time and false noses', in *Rethinking Anthropology.* London: Athlone Press, 132–6.

Leach, E. R. (1976), *Culture and Communication.* Cambridge: Cambridge University Press.

Lévi-Strauss, C. (1978), *Myth and Meaning.* London: Routledge & Kegan Paul.

Lewis, G. (1980), *Day of Shining Red: An Essay on Understanding Ritual.* Cambridge: Cambridge University Press.

Lewis, M. A. (2007), 'Towards a systematic spirituality of black British women'. Unpublished PhD thesis, University of Birmingham.

Lincoln, B. (1996) 'Gendered discourses: the early history of "mythos" and "logos"', *History of Religions,* 36, (1), 1–12.

Livezey, L. (ed.) (2000), *Public Religion and Urban Transformation: Faith in the City*. New York: New York University Press.

Low, S. M. and Lawrence-Zúñiga, D. (eds) (2003), *The Anthropology of Space and Place: Locating Culture*. Oxford: Blackwell Publishing.

Lowie, R. H. (1936), *Primitive Religion*. London: Routledge.

Lynch, G. (2005), *Understanding Theology and Popular Culture*. Oxford: Blackwell.

Malinowski, B. (1922), *Argonauts of the Western Pacific: An Account of Native Enterprise and Adventure in the Archipelagoes of Melanesian New Guinea*. London: Routledge and Kegan Paul.

Malinowski, B. (1967), *A Diary in the Strict Sense of the Term*. London: Routledge and Kegan Paul.

Martin, D. (1990), *Tongues of Fire: The Explosion of Protestantism in Latin America*. Oxford: Blackwell.

Masuzawa, T. (2005), *The Invention of World Religions, or How European Universalism was Preserved in the Language of Pluralism*. Chicago: University of Chicago Press.

McDannell, C. (1995), 'Creating the Christian home: home schooling in contemporary America', in D. Chidester and E. T. Linenthal (eds), *American Sacred Space*. Bloomington: Indiana University Press.

McGuire, M. B. (1997), 'Mapping contemporary American spirituality: a sociological perspective', *Christian Spirituality Bulletin* 5, (1), 1–8.

Meskell, L. and Pels, P. (eds) (2005), *Embedding Ethics*. Oxford: Berg.

Milbank, J. (1990), *Theology and Social Theory: Beyond Secular Reason*. Oxford: Blackwell.

Moore, R. (1974), *Pit-Men, Preachers and Politics: The Effects of Methodism in a Durham Mining Community*. Cambridge: Cambridge University Press.

Morphy, H. (1998), 'Spencer and Gillen in Durkheim: the theoretical construction of ethnography', in N. J. Allen, W. S. F. Pickering and W. Watts Miller (eds), *On Durkheim's Elementary Forms of Religious Life*. London: Routledge, 13–28.

Morris, B. (1987), *Anthropological Studies of Religion: An Introductory Text*. Cambridge: Cambridge University Press.

Morris, B. (2006), *Religion and Anthropology: A Critical Introduction*. Cambridge: Cambridge University Press.

Mumford, L. S. (1995), *Love and Ideology in the Afternoon: Soap Opera, Women and Television Genre.* Bloomington: Indiana University Press.

Nagle, R. (1997), *Claiming the Virgin: The Broken Promise of Liberation Theology in Brazil.* New York: Routledge.

Okley, J. (1996), *Own or Other Culture.* London: Routledge.

Otto, R. (1928), *The Idea of the Holy: An Inquiry into the Non-Rational Factor in the Idea of the Divine and its Relation to the Rational.* Oxford: Oxford University Press.

Ozorak, E. W. (1996), 'The power but not the glory: how women empower themselves through religion', *Journal for the Scientific Study of Religion* 35, (1), 17–29.

Pearson, J. (2002), '"Going native in reverse": the insider as researcher in British Wicca', in E. Arweck and M. D. Stringer (eds), *Theorizing Faith, The Insider/Outsider Problem in the Study of Ritual.* Birmingham: University of Birmingham Press, 97–114.

Pouillon, J. (1982), 'Remarks on the verb "to believe"', in M. Izard and P. Smith (eds), *Between Belief and Transgression.* Chicago: University of Chicago Press, 1–8.

Pratt, M. L. (1986), 'Fieldwork in common places', in J. Clifford and G. F. Marcus (eds), *Writing Culture: The Poetics and Politics of Ethnography.* Berkley: University of California Press, 27–50.

Punch, M. (1986), *The Politics and Ethics of Fieldwork.* London: Sage.

Radway, J. (1984), *Reading the Romance: Women, Patriarchy and Popular Literature.* Chapel Hill: University of North Carolina Press.

Ramp, W. (1998), 'Effervescence, differentiation and representation in *The Elementary Forms*', in N. J. Allen, W. S. F. Pickering and W. Watts Miller (eds), *On Durkheim's Elementary Forms of Religious Life.* London: Routledge, 136–48.

Redfield, R. (1960), *Peasant Society and Culture.* Chicago: University of Chicago Press.

Richards, A. (1956), *Chisungu: A Girl's Initiation Rite among the Bemba of Northern Rhodesia.* London: Faber and Faber.

Robertson Smith, W. (1894), *Lectures on the Religion of the Semites.* London: Adam and Charles Black.

Rosaldo, R. (1986), 'From the door of his tent: the fieldworker and the inquisitor', in J. Clifford and G. F. Marcus (eds), *Writing Culture: The*

*Poetics and Politics of Ethnography*. Berkley: University of California Press, 77–97.

Royal Anthropological Institute (1971), *Notes and Queries on Anthropology*. London: Routledge and Kegan Paul.

Sahlins, M. (1974), *Stone Age Economics*. London: Tavistock.

Schofield, S. (1999), 'What is the role of worship, and decisions made about it in the lives of those living in urban priority areas, with particular reference to the experience of power and powerlessness?' Unpublished MPhil thesis, University of Birmingham.

Smart, N. (1989), *The World's Religions*. Cambridge: Cambridge University Press.

Smith, J. H. (2005), 'Mary in the kitchen, Martha in the pew: patterns of holiness in a Methodist Church'. Unpublished MPhil thesis, University of Birmingham.

Smith, J. Z. (1987), *To Take Place: Toward Theory in Ritual*. Chicago: University of Chicago Press.

Smith, J. Z. (1998), 'Religion, religions, religious', in M. C. Taylor (ed.), *Critical Terms for Religions Studies*. Chicago: Chicago University Press, 269–84.

Smith, J. Z. (2000), 'Classification', in W. Braun and R. T. McCutcheon (eds), *Guide to the Study of Religion*. London: Cassell, 35–43.

Southwold, M. (1978) 'Buddhism and the definition of religion', *Man* (NS), 13, 362–79.

Southwold, M. (1983), *Buddhism in Life, The Anthropological Study of Religion and the Sinhalese Practice of Buddhism*. Manchester: Manchester University Press.

Sperber, D. (1974), *Rethinking Symbolism*. Cambridge: Cambridge University Press.

Sperber, D. (1982), 'Is symbolic thought prerational?', in M. Izard and P. Smith (eds), *Between Belief and Transgression*. Chicago: University of Chicago Press, 245–64.

Spiro, M. E. (1966), 'Religion: problems of definition and explanation', in M. Banton (ed.), *Anthropological Approaches to the Study of Religion*. London: Tavistock, 85–126.

Stocking, G. W. (1983), 'The ethnographer's magic: fieldwork in British anthropology from Tylor to Malinowski', in G. W. Stocking (ed.), *Observers Observed: Essays on Ethnographic Fieldwork*. Madison: University of Wisconsin Press, 70–120.

Stocking, G. W. (1995), *After Tylor: British Social Anthropology 1888–1951*. Madison: University of Wisconsin Press.

Strathern, M. (1981), *Kinship at the Core: An Anthropology of Elmdon, A Village in North-West Essex in the 1960s*. Cambridge: Cambridge University Press.

Strauss, A. and Corbin, J. (1990), *Basics of Qualitative Research*. London: Sage.

Strenski, I. (2006), *Thinking About Religion: An Historical Introduction to Theories of Religion*. Oxford: Blackwell.

Stringer, M. D. (1996), 'Towards a situational theory of belief', *Journal of the Anthropological Society of Oxford*, xxvii, (3), 217–34.

Stringer, M. D. (1999a), *On the Perception of Worship: The Ethnography of Worship in Four Christian Congregations in Manchester*. Birmingham: University of Birmingham Press.

Stringer, M. D. (1999b), 'Rethinking animism: thoughts from the infancy of our discipline', *Journal of the Royal Anthropological Institute* (NS) 5, (4), 541–56.

Stringer, M. D. (2002), 'Introduction: theorizing faith', in E. Arweck and M. D. Stringer (eds), *Theorizing Faith: The Insider/Outsider Problem in the Study of Ritual*. Birmingham: University of Birmingham Press, 1–20.

Stringer, M. D. (2004), 'Identity and the Anglican priesthood: debates on the ordination of women and homosexuals in sociological perspective', in S. Coleman and P. Collins (eds), *Religion, Identity and Change: Perspectives on Global Transformations*. Aldershot: Ashgate, 57–68.

Stringer, M. D. (2005), *A Sociological History of Christian Worship*. Cambridge: Cambridge University Press.

Sugirtharajah, S. (2003), *Imagining Hinduism: A Postcolonial Perspective*. London: Routledge.

Sutherland, S. (1988), 'The study of religion and religions', in S. Sutherland and P. Clark (eds), *The World's Religions: The Study of Religion, Traditional and New Religion*. London: Routledge, 29–40.

Tambiah, S. J. (1990), *Magic, Science, Religion and the Scope of Rationality*. Cambridge: Cambridge University Press.

Taussig, M. (1987), *Shamanism, Colonialism and the Wild Man: A Study in Terror and Healing.* Chicago: University of Chicago Press.

Taylor, C. (1991), *The Ethics of Authenticity.* Cambridge: Harvard University Press.

Turner, V. (1967), *The Forest of Symbols: Aspects of Ndembu Ritual.* Ithaca: Cornell University Press.

Turner, V. (1968), *The Drums of Affliction: A Study of Religious Processes among the Ndembu of Zambia.* London: Hutchinson.

Turner, V. (1969), *The Ritual Process: Structure and Anti-Structure.* Harmondsworth: Penguin.

Tylor, E. B. (1871), *Primitive Culture: Researches into the Development of Mythology, Philosophy, Religion, Art and Custom.* London: John Murray.

Van Gennep, A. (1960), *The Rites of Passage.* London: Routledge and Kegan Paul.

Varisco, D. M. (2005), *Islam Obscured: The Rhetoric of Anthropological Representation.* New York: Palgrave Macmillan.

Wagner, R. (1981), *The Invention of Culture.* Chicago: University of Chicago Press.

Williams, D. S. (1993), *Sisters in the Wilderness: The Challenge of Womanist God-Talk.* Maryknoll: Orbis.

Williams, S. (1999), *Religious Belief and Popular Culture in Southwark, c.1880–1939.* Oxford: Oxford University Press.

Woodhead, L. (2002), 'Women and religion', in L. Woodhead *et al* (eds), *Religions in the Modern World.* London: Routledge, 332–56.

Wulff, R. M. and Fiske, S. J. (eds) (1987), *Anthropological Praxis: Translating Knowledge into Action.* Boulder: Westview Press.

Wuthnow, R. (1994), *Sharing the Journey: Support Groups and America's New Quest for Community.* New York: The Free Press.

Young, M. and Willmott, P. (1957), *Family and Kinship in East London.* London: Routledge and Kegan Paul.

Young, M. W. (1979), 'Introduction', in M. W. Young (ed.), *The Ethnography of Malinowski: The Trobriand Islands 1915–1918.* London: Routledge and Kegan Paul.

# Index